IMPROVE YOUR BUSINESS

HANDBOOK

IMPROVE YOUR BUSINESS

Edited by D. E. N. Dickson

HANDBOOK

International Labour Office · Geneva

This publication was developed by the Improve Your Business project of the Management Development Branch of the International Labour Office, with financial assistance from the Swedish International Development Authority (SIDA), from an original idea conceived by the Swedish Employers' Confederation and published in *Se Om Ditt Företag* (Stockholm, 1974). A preliminary test edition was published by the ILO in 1981.

Dickson, D. E. N.
Improve your business: Handbook
Geneva, International Labour Office, 1986

/Guide/, /Management/, /Small enterprise/s. 12.04.1
ISBN 92-2-105341-5
ISBN for complete set of two volumes 92-2-105342-3
Also published in Spanish: *Mejore su negocio. Manual* (ISBN 92-2-305341-2; ISBN for complete set of two volumes 92-2-305342-0), Geneva, 1990

ILO Cataloguing in Publication Data

ILO publications can be obtained through major booksellers or ILO local offices in many countries, or direct from ILO Publications, International Labour Office, CH-1211 Geneva 22, Switzerland. A catalogue or list of new publications will be sent free of charge from the above address.

FOREWORD

In recent years there has been an upsurge of interest in the role of small-scale enterprises as providers of employment and contributors to gross national product, and as a key component in economic development. This has been accompanied by the corresponding appearance of numerous publications on how to run small businesses. Given this, what is the justification for another book on the subject?

There are few publications which are simple enough to be understood easily by people with limited formal education but which can still communicate all the basic management knowledge required by entrepreneurs if they are to run small businesses successfully. This book is an attempt to fill this gap.

The underlying idea of the book is that improvements can best come from active and creative thinking by entrepreneurs about their own businesses. The purpose of this material is therefore to encourage such creative thinking and motivate entrepreneurs to take action to improve their businesses.

The material can be used equally well by individual business people or by trainers giving small business seminars and workshops.

The writing and publication of this book, as well as field testing of earlier versions in eastern Africa, was made possible by financial assistance from the Swedish International Development Authority (SIDA). The main author and editor of this edition of *Improve your business* is D. E. N. Dickson, ILO Chief Technical Adviser in Nairobi. He was assisted by Henny Romijn and Per Linden. Many of the ideas in the *Handbook* and *Workbook* owe their origin to the earlier work of the late Rhys Wynne-Roberts, who devoted so much time and effort to adapting the original idea conceived by the Swedish Employers' Confederation. Acknowledgement is also due to many other colleagues in the ILO Management Development Branch, the Kenya Industrial Estates and other organisations, for the comments and suggestions on how to focus and present this material.

CONTENTS

WHAT IS *IMPROVE YOUR BUSINESS?*

Improve your business is about running small businesses. It has been written for retailers, wholesalers, manufacturers and operators of services such as repair services, laundries, dry cleaners and restaurants. Although in a small book like this we cannot hope to deal with the special conditions of each different trade, most of what we say can be used in many different trades or branches of industry. We have given examples from trade, manufacturing and service industries.

Improve your business is material for you to work with. It comes in two parts: a *Handbook,* which you are reading now, and a *Workbook.* They are best read together but they can each be useful if read separately. We recommend that you start using the *Workbook* and when needed turn to the *Handbook* for assistance.

Both the *Handbook* and the *Workbook* consist of eight sections, each of which deals with an important part of the management of your business. Each section of the *Handbook* has a corresponding section in the *Workbook.* The sections stand on their own and can be read separately.

▲ IMPROVE YOUR
BUSINESS IS FOR:

RETAILERS

WHOLESALERS

MANUFACTURERS

**OPERATORS
OF SERVICES**

THE HANDBOOK

The *Handbook* talks very simply about some of the important things that you must know and understand if you are to make your business work well over a long time. It is not a textbook, but you can get some interesting and useful ideas from the *Handbook.* The sections are set out in the same order as the sections in the *Workbook,* so that you can easily go from *Workbook* to *Handbook* or from *Handbook* to *Workbook.*

GIVES YOU
MANAGEMENT
IDEAS

THE WORKBOOK

The *Workbook* will make you think hard about your business; it will do this by asking you a number of questions about your business and the way you are running it. In each section of the *Workbook* there is a list of simple questions to which you answer "yes" or "no". The answers you write will tell you how much you know about the strengths and weaknesses of your business.

TELLS YOU YOUR STRENGTHS AND WEAKNESSES

The *Workbook* will also give you the possibility of learning more about the financial and practical sides of the business by means of simple exercises in business practice.

If you want to improve your management skills after going through the *Workbook*, you should then read the management ideas which we put in the *Handbook*.

WHERE TO START

We recommend that you start by going through the section which deals with that part of management which you think is weakest in your business.

If you do not know the strong and weak points in the management of your business, you can find this out by filling in the sheet called "Finding out your strengths and weaknesses" which is placed behind the introductory section, "For you in business". We advise you to fill in this sheet before you start using *Improve your business.*

> *Note :* Since this book is intended for use in many different countries, we have used the term "NU" in the examples to represent an imaginary "*n*ational *u*nit of currency".

FOR YOU
IN BUSINESS

It is for you in business that we have written *Improve your business*. Why? Because every business has scope for improving its sales and profits.

Even if your business is already doing very well, there are always things which can be done in a better way which you may not have thought of.

It is *you*, as the owner/manager, who has to make those improvements. You are the person who is responsible for everything that goes well and for everything that goes wrong in your business. You are also the one who sets the example to your employees.

All this means that you have to understand the working of your business very well, and also that you must be capable of putting that knowledge to good use by applying it in the actual management of your business. This is where *Improve your business* can help you. When you go through this *Handbook* you will acquire all the basic knowledge which you require to succeed in business. At the same time you will find that the material can help you to improve your management skills so that you can put your management ideas into practice.

YOUR AIMS IN BUSINESS

Before you start reading *Improve your business,* sit down for a while and think carefully about your business. Ask yourself what your *aims* are. Do you know exactly what you want to achieve with your business? Have you thought of what your activities in the market should be? Whom do you want to reach with your products or services? Do you know who your competitors are? Do you produce your goods or services in the most efficient way? Where do you want to go with your business in the future?

Having a clear idea about your goals in business is very important when you plan your business activities. Only if you know where you want to go will you make good use of your resources and be successful in business.

YOU AND YOUR BUSINESS

To run any business means that you gather together things and people and put them to work to earn money for you. These things may be in the form of your own personal skill, the money you have saved, borrowed money, machines and raw materials and the skills of the people who work for you. If you are to earn your living from the business, then you must employ these things and people in a good way. This means that you must learn to think of these things and people as a separate group of assets called "the business". The business assets must be kept separate from your own private assets and from the members of your family.

BUSINESS AND **FAMILY**: KEEP THEM **SEPARATE**

THE BUSINESS AND PROFIT

The major objective for being in business is to make a profit (or "a surplus", as some people prefer to say). Profit is made when the money which flows into your business is greater than the money which flows out. The greater the difference between *money in* and *money out,* the greater is the *profit*.

HOW PROFIT IS MADE

1. Money <u>in</u> from sales

2. Money <u>out</u> for costs

3. Profit is what is left

REMEMBER:

SALES 100

LESS

COSTS 80

GIVES

PROFIT 20

Now you know how profit is made:

Money <u>in</u> — **Money <u>out</u>** = **Profit**

YOU AND *IMPROVE YOUR BUSINESS*

If you read the ideas in this *Handbook* and think about them, you will know how to do two things:

1. You will know simple techniques which will help you to expand your market and increase your *sales.* Your sales will grow bigger, as you can see below:

***More* money <u>in</u>** — **Money <u>out</u>** = ***More* profit**

2. You will understand what are the various types of *costs* which your firm will have to pay. By understanding these costs you will be able to keep them under control and maybe even cut some of them.

If you can learn to do this even in a small way, you will control the money which flows out of your business. Your costs will become smaller.

In these ways you will earn a greater surplus or profit from your business and you will make your business more successful.

More and more money in   –   **Smaller money out**   =   **Even more profit**

FINDING OUT YOUR STRENGTHS AND WEAKNESSES

Before you start using *Improve your business,* you may wish to find out about your performance in business. You can get a rough idea about your strengths and weaknesses by answering the questions below. Each question concerns one area of management and corresponds to one particular section of *Improve your business.* For example, question 1 corresponds to section 1, question 2 to section 2 and so forth. Find out from your answers in which area(s) of management you are weakest and start reading the corresponding sections of *Improve your business.*

How good are you at...	Good	Average	Bad
1. Buying, selling and stock control?	☐	☐	☐
2. Production management and production technology?	☐	☐	☐
3. Bookkeeping?	☐	☐	☐
4. Costing and pricing your products or services?	☐	☐	☐
5. Marketing?	☐	☐	☐
6. Management accounting?	☐	☐	☐
7. Planning your business activities?	☐	☐	☐
8. Organising your office?	☐	☐	☐

BUYING AND SELLING

All businesses must buy and sell to make a *profit*. The profit is made by buying at a low price and selling at a higher price.

- Good *selling* can increase your *sales*
- Good *buying* can decrease your *costs*
- This means : *bigger profit*

Retail and wholesale traders buy goods at a low price which they store, pack and distribute to sell at a higher price. This is the way they make a profit. They can work out whether they have made a profit (or a loss) in this way :

	Sales of goods		500
Less :	Buying costs of goods		300
	Difference or gross profit		200
Less :	Other costs		
	Rent of shop	60	
	Wages	100	160
	Surplus or net profit		40

Manufacturers buy materials and parts which they make into goods using labour, machines and power. They then sell the goods at prices which must be higher than their total costs. This is the way they make a profit.

Service operators sell services such as transport, repairing or cleaning. Like manufacturers, they use labour, machines and equipment and sometimes vehicles, fuel and power. The prices they charge for their services must be higher than their total costs. This is the way they make a profit.

Manufacturers and service operators can work out whether they have made a profit (or a loss) in this way:

	Sales of goods or services		500
Less:	Buying costs		
	Raw materials	150	
	Labour	100	250
	Difference or gross profit		250
Less:	Other costs		
	Rent for workshop	60	
	Salaries and office costs	75	135
	Surplus or net profit		115

SELLING

The more you know about your customers and what they want, the more you will sell and the bigger can be your profit.

RETAIL AND WHOLESALE SELLING

The first step towards increasing your sales is to attract more people into your shop or store. Then, encourage them to stay and examine your goods, so that they buy as much as possible. To do this, your shop must be:

- well lit;
- clean and fresh looking;
- nicely decorated; and
- with the goods well displayed.

You should also have an attractive sign outside. None of these things take much money but they *do* help to increase your sales.

To sell their goods well, traders must:

- know who their customers are; and
- make sure they have the goods of the quality the customers want at prices they can afford to pay.

AN ATTRACTIVE
SHOP IS:

WELL LIT

**CLEAN AND
FRESH-LOOKING**

NICELY DECORATED

WITH THE **GOODS
WELL DISPLAYED**

WITH **AN
EYE-CATCHING
SIGN OUTSIDE**

8

Customers must be able to see the goods they want. Sometimes retailers can make people buy the goods they want to sell by putting them at the front of their counters.

If your stocks of some goods are low, put them to the back of the shop. The people who really want them will ask. The others will not see them.

WHAT CUSTOMERS
SEE, THEY WANT
TO BUY

Try to write down those goods which sell well and those which do not. In this way, you will understand better your customers' wants and you will not waste money buying goods which you cannot easily sell.

If there are other retailers selling the same goods as you in the town or in the market, go and see from time to time what they are selling. See whether—

- their prices are the same as or higher or lower than yours;

- their goods are better set out and easier to see;

- they have some articles which you do not have;

- the goods are of better quality than yours.

If you think some other shops do better than you, don't just copy them–*do better still.*

GET IDEAS
FROM COMPETITORS

INDUSTRIAL SELLING

Manufacturers or operators of services who know their markets well are more likely to be successful than those who do not know very much about their markets.

The most successful business people are those who study the market and set out to meet its demands.

What does your market look like?

You must find answers to the following questions:

- what the products are;
- who the customers are;
- where the customers are;

- how many customers you hope to sell to; and
- how much they buy.

Find out the answers to these questions by doing simple market research. Do the following:

- talk to your customers;

- ask what they like;

- look at competitors;

- look at what people buy;

- get information about your products or services.

▲ **MARKET RESEARCH MEANS:**

LOOK, ASK, TALK AND GET INFORMATION

Offer something different from your competitors, such as different sizes, different colours or different packaging. But do not be too different unless you are sure that it will sell.

BUYING TO SELL

Before you can sell you must buy. How well you will sell depends on how well you have bought.

Intelligent buying can reduce your costs and make more profit for your business.

RETAIL AND WHOLESALE BUYING

Before you can buy you must know to whom you are selling and the sort of goods they want. As you have read in the section on selling: *You must know your customers.* For a retailer or wholesaler, intelligent buying means to buy goods:

GOOD BUYING
MEANS

RIGHT TYPES
AND SIZE

- of the *types* and *sizes* that your customers want;

- at *buying prices* which are low enough for you to add a reasonable profit, while your customers are able to afford your selling prices;

- in *quantities* such that you have the goods in stock when needed, but not so many that your money is tied up for a long time.

RIGHT PRICES

If you are a small trader, you may have to buy in small quantities. Big traders who buy in big quantities can buy from manufacturers or get big discounts from wholesalers, but on small quantities you cannot get discounts. You may even have to buy from other retailers. Your profits will be small.

RIGHT QUANTITIES

You may even be tied to one supplier who gives you credit. Even if you know that other suppliers' goods are better or cheaper, you cannot go to them because you are always in debt.

There is no easy way out of this. You already work very hard but this is not enough. You must use your brains.

Be hard on yourself and your family. Save every NU you can until you have enough to pay cash for your supplies and can choose your supplier.

Once you are free to choose your supplier, find out the ones who can give you what your customers will buy— and make sure you know what they want.

Compare what different suppliers can offer in the way of:

- prices;
- delivery;
- discounts;
- credit;
- quality; and
- something different.

**DON'T BE TIED
TO ONE SUPPLIER,**

Choose the supplier who gives you the best in terms of prices, quality and delivery.

COMPARE
SUPPLIERS!

INDUSTRIAL BUYING

For manufacturers or operators of services, the way they do their buying has a big influence on whether their businesses are profitable. If they buy well, their prices can be lower, the quality will be better and they will be more competitive.

One way in which you can improve your buying is to break down your purchases into three groups as follows:

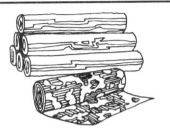  

- **Raw materials (wood for the carpenter, cloth for the tailor)**
- **Manufactured parts (locks, buttons for shirts)**
- **Equipment for your own use (tools, etc.)**

Raw materials need not be stored in your own store-room. You can often make a special arrangement with your supplier so that you can have the raw materials delivered just when you need them. In this way, you do not tie up money for storage. If raw materials are in your store-room too long, sell them off even at cost price. Manufactured parts are often cheaper if they are bought in larger quantities. If you can buy one dozen, this will be cheaper than if you buy one single item.

Can you buy bigger quantities jointly with other people and get a discount for quantity?

Tools and other equipment for your own use must always be available. When they are broken, replace them immediately.

SINGLE ITEM:
HIGH PRICE PER ITEM

ONE DOZEN ITEMS:
LOW PRICE PER ITEM

HOW TO BUY

1. Examine your needs

THINK!

- **How much do I need?**
- **What quality do I need?**
- **What price do I pay?**
- **When do I need the goods?**

2. Find the supplier

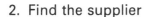

- **Look in telephone book**
- **Ask friends in trade**
- **Look in trade directory**
- **Contact Chamber of Commerce**

3. Ask for quotations from several suppliers

- **Telephone them**
- **Write to them**
- **Visit them**
- **Get written quotations**

4. Negotiate terms and then buy

- **Talk with each supplier**
- **Compare their prices**
- **Ask for lower prices**
- **Ask for discount**

5. On the day the goods arrive, *check* quantity, quality and price against delivery note

- **Check all deliveries**
- **Examine their condition**
- **Check the delivery notes**
- **Check the storage**

6. If you have any complaints, complain to the supplier immediately

- **Contact the supplier himself**
- **Explain the problem**
- **Ask for a solution**
- **Get it in writing**

7. Check your invoices against the delivery note when it arrives

- **Check the prices**
- **Check the quantities**
- **Check the discounts**
- **Check the additions**

Lastly, there are always new materials, parts and tools being introduced. *Keep yourself up to date.*

STOCK CONTROL

Stock control means keeping a check on your stock of goods, materials and parts. With good stock control you can:

- **make sure you do not run out of stock;**

- **make sure you do not hold too much stock of any item.**

Why your business can run out of stock:

- because you have forgotten to order goods or materials to replace those sold or used:

- because you have ordered too late;

- because you did not know stocks were low.

TOO LITTLE STOCK

Why it is bad to run out of stock:

- because if you run out of stock and must say "no" to customers, they may go to competitors and may not come back to you again.

Why your business can hold too much stock:

- because you do not know which of your goods are not selling well, and stocks are piling up;

- because you do not know how much stock you have, if your stock is not easy to see and count;

- because you do not check regularly how much stock you have in your store.

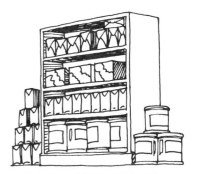

TOO MUCH STOCK

Why it is bad to hold too much stock:

- because if you keep much larger quantities of stock than you need, you have tied up money which you could be using more profitably.

THE RULES OF STOCK CONTROL

RULE 1 – CHECK YOUR STOCKS REGULARLY

How often you do so—once a month, once a week or even once a day—depends on your type of business, how fast your stocks move and how much stock you keep. If you keep your stocks at low levels because you want to keep down the amount of money tied up, you must check often.

Take note of goods and materials which are selling fast

CHECK STOCKS
REGULARLY

and those which are selling slowly.

RULE 2 – SET OUT YOUR STOCKS WELL SO THAT THEY
ARE EASY TO SEE AND COUNT

If the stocks are mixed up, they will not be easy to see
and will be very difficult to count.

Stocks mixed up   **Stocks well set out**

SET OUT
STOCKS WELL

RULE 3 – AS THE NUMBER OF STOCK ITEMS
INCREASES, SET THEM OUT IN THEIR
SEPARATE GROUPS

Dresses must be stored by type of dress, model and
size. The sizes must be clearly marked. Items such as
cans of paint must be set out by maker, size, if there is
more than one size (1/2 litre, 1 litre, 2 litres, etc.), and
colour.

Small items – screws, nuts, washers, fuses and so
on–may be kept in small boxes, one for each article
and size. The name must be marked on each box
(e.g. Brass screw, 4 mm × 30 mm). The boxes must be
stored by item and size. Whatever stock control system
you use, your shelves and stock room must be kept in
order.

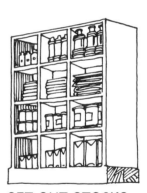

SET OUT STOCKS
BY SIZE

If you have only a few different stock items, you will
not need written stock records. You can simply look at
the separate groups, count them and see whether you
need to reorder some items, or whether you have
overstocked some goods which are not selling.

RULE 4 – WHEN THE NUMBER OF STOCK ITEMS
GROWS TO MORE THAN 20, KEEP SIMPLE
WRITTEN STOCK RECORDS

When you have many stock items, it takes too much
time to count them. They will also be difficult to find.
Write them into a book or on cards. Read the next
section to find out how.

KEEP STOCK
RECORDS

15

UNIT STOCK CONTROL

Manufacturers as well as service operators and retailers can use a unit stock control system. This type of stock control is called *unit stock control* because it shows the number of units or articles which are in stock. Under this system you have a card for each of the different types of stock.

Here is an example of a stock card for retailers. The system works in exactly the same way for a manufacturer or service operator.

Article : batteries			Reorder level : 100	
Cost price : 20				
Selling price : 22.50			STOCK CARD	
Date	Particulars	Stock in	Stock out	Balance
1 June	Purchased	200	–	200
3 June	Sold		20	180
4 June	Sold		20	160
8 June	Sold		30	130
11 June	Sold		10	120
16 June	Sold		20	100 Reorder !

Each time you buy or sell batteries, you enter the date and particulars on the card.

The Balance column is adjusted to show how many batteries are still in stock.

When do you reorder your batteries?
To find out, you must know–

● how many batteries you sell every week or every month;

● how long it takes you to get delivery of batteries.

You find from the above stock card that you sell 40 batteries each week. Your supplier can deliver the batteries one week after you have given him your order. Therefore, you should order when your stock is 100 or below. This gives you 40 in hand for the week's delay and 60 more in case they do not come on time or you sell more than 40 in the next week. So 100 is your *reorder level*.

REORDER WHEN 100 LEFT

VALUE STOCK CONTROL

If you are a retail trader you can use a simple stock control system which tells you the *total value* of all the goods which you have in stock rather than the number of units.

In all shops, goods are purchased at a lower price—*the cost price*—and resold at a higher price—*the selling price.* When you keep stock records, you want to know *either* how much your business would get if all the goods than are in stock were sold, *or* how much has been paid by you in total for all the goods in stock.

The easiest method is to record the value of all your stock at *selling price.* It is easier to use selling prices since they are marked on the goods which customers buy and they are used when sales are recorded.

The easiest way to record your stock is to use a stock control book as below:

Stock control book			
Month: January 1986			
Date	Particulars	Increase in stock (value in)	Decrease in stock (value out)	Balance stock in hand (value)
1 Jan.	Opening stock			43,250
2 Jan.	Sales		3,200	40,050
3 Jan.	Purchase			
	Goods Ltd.	3,000		43,050

The entries in the book are the same as the entries on the stock cards above, except for the fact that the entries are made in value instead of units.

SOME SPECIAL SITUATIONS

Some items, such as wooden planks, steel rods, sheets of metal and bolts of cloth, are difficult to count quickly and easily. In these cases, the solution is to have a *bin card*. This card contains all the information needed about the item, and is kept with each item on the rack, shelf and so on.

Every movement, in or out, of the item is recorded on the card. When the *reorder level* is approached, you reorder the item. Note the hole at the top—it can be tied to a nail or drawer handle.

USE **BIN CARDS** FOR SPECIAL ITEMS

No. 62 ○ **BIN CARD**			
Name: Steel bars			
Unit: Metre			
Reorder at 2,000 metres			
Date	In	Out	In stock
13 Oct.			3,200
14 Oct.		1,000	2,200
18 Oct.		700	1,500 reorder!
22 Oct.	5,000		6,500

Small items, such as nails, washers and so on, are very tedious to count. One way of handling them is to count out or weigh out the reorder level quantity into a paper or plastic bag, and put the bag at the back of the drawer, shelf or bin. When you have to open the bag to serve a customer, you know it is time to reorder.

Slow-moving stocks take up space that you may want for goods which sell well. Try to sell them off as special offers at reduced prices.

WHEN YOU OPEN THE BAG: REORDER!

If they are very old, sell them off at cost price or give them away.

HANDLING CASH

You must know exactly how much cash you take in and how much you give out — and how you spend it.

A simple way to control your cash is as follows:

1. Count your amount of money when the business opens in the morning. Whenever you take in cash, put it in the drawer. Each time you pay out cash, write out a cash voucher.

MORNING: 100

2. Count the amount of cash again at the end of the business day.

EVENING: 300

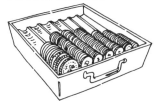

3. The difference between the amount in the morning and the amount in the evening is called your *net takings*.

NET TAKINGS: 200

4. Add up your cash vouchers. This gives the *total cash paid out* during the day. Remember that this cash has been taken from the cash drawer, and so must be added on to the net takings to show the total cash which has come into the business during the day.

5. Add the total of the vouchers to your net takings. This gives you the *total cash* which has come in from sales during the day.

TOTAL **CASH VOUCHERS PAID OUT:**

20 + 15 + 35 = 70.

	Vouchers	70
plus:	Net takings	200
	Total cash in from sales during the day	270

HOW TO CONTROL CASH

It is easier to control the cash coming in and the cash going out if you write down the details of every sale and payment in a *cash book*.

If you have a bank account, you can also add columns for *Bank in* and *Bank out*.

Your cash book can look as follows:

Date	Details	Cash in	Cash out	Bank in	Bank out
1 Mar.	Cash at start	100			
1 Mar.	Cash sale	150			
1 Mar.	Toilet rolls		20		
1 Mar.	Typewriter ribbons		15		
1 Mar.	Cash sale	120			
1 Mar.	To bank		35	35	
		370	70	35	
Less:	Cash at start	100			
Less:	Total money from sales	270			
	Cash out	70			
	Net cash in	200			

THE CASH REGISTER

If you are a retail trader you should keep a cash register which you or an honest employee or member of your own family operates. One person should be in charge of both cash going out of and cash coming into the cash register. The business cash must be kept separate from your own cash and the cash of members of your family.

By keeping the cash register paper rolls, you can see what you take in and give out every day, week, month or year. It is good to see how money comes in and is paid out over a long time because business may change from day to day. One day it may be very good, the next day bad. Compare your business result of this month with that of last month.

KEEP THE **CASH REGISTER PAPER ROLLS**

THE RULES OF CASH CONTROL

1. Do not allow members of the family to take cash from the business unless it is their wage, it is given by you *and they sign a receipt for it.*

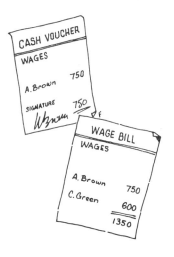

2. Pay yourself and each member of the family working in the business regular wages which you can charge to the business like those of your other employees. This can help you to have more control over the outflow of your cash.

3. Decide on how much you can draw each week as a salary for yourself, but keep it low. Remember, you must also put aside money to buy stocks, pay wages, replace old machinery, pay taxes and so on. You must also have something left over in reserve in case business is bad or you want to make it bigger. This is the only way you can build up capital and improve your business.

4. If you or a member of your family takes goods from the shop or the business—a can of food or a piece of clothing, for example—put the money into the cash box.

5. Make sure that you have enough money in the bank to meet the normal needs of the business.

GOOD BOOKKEEPING

As your business grows and you buy and sell more of different goods, you need more information from your accounts. Therefore bookkeeping is important. To know more about it, read the Bookkeeping section of the *Handbook*. If you want to set up a bookkeeping system, you may get help from your local Small Business Centre or you may hire someone. This means that you must save all your bills, invoices, cash register rolls and other papers about money to give him when he comes.

And last, but not least, once again : Keep your own and your family's hands out of the business cash !

REMEMBER:
TAKE CARE
OF YOUR CASH!

KEEP ALL HANDS
OUT OF THE
CASH DRAWER!

MANUFACTURING AND SERVICE OPERATING

2

MANUFACTURING

Manufacturing means processing and/or assembling raw materials and sometimes parts to make them into products, using workers (labour), machines, tools and power.

The raw materials (wood, steel, cloth, chemicals, etc.) and the parts (handles, nails, screws, wire, thread, etc.), as well as the labour and the power, are called *inputs* because they are put into the making of the products.

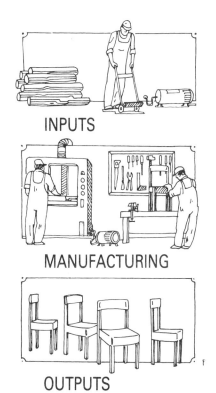

INPUTS

MANUFACTURING

Products are the goods which are *manufactured* or produced in a workshop or factory.

OUTPUTS

The quantities of products produced by a business during a period of time are called the *outputs.*

THE STAGES OF MANUFACTURING

The stages of manufacturing always follow one another in the same order, whatever the products may be.

STAGE 1 – STORING

The materials and parts which have been bought arrive in the raw material store. They are checked and stored till needed.

STAGE 2 – PROCESSING

The raw materials are processed, for example by cutting, sawing, machining or sewing.

STAGE 3 – ASSEMBLING

The parts are put together to make a product (i.e. assembly takes place). Where the product is simple – flour, cotton yarn or steel bars – assembly does not take place.

STAGE 4 – FINISHING

Finishing takes place. This includes, for example, painting, polishing, washing, dyeing or glueing.

STAGE 5 – INSPECTION

Inspection takes place to check that the product has been made correctly and is ready to be sent to the customer. This is a check for quality.

STAGE 6 – PACKING

The product is packed, ready to be sent to the customer.

Each stage of manufacturing involves costs. Some of these costs are unavoidable, as you need raw materials, labour and energy to manufacture your product. But in manufacturing businesses the amount of money spent on these items is often greater than it should be. This leads to high costs. The main causes of these high costs are:

● waste of raw materials;

● waste of workers' time;

● waste of machine time;

● waste by tying up too much working capital.

It is important that your goods are produced with the smallest possible waste. Waste adds to the cost of the product and reduces the possible profit.

The cheaper you can produce, the cheaper you can sell, so that:

● more people buy your goods; and

● you are more able to compete with other manufacturers.

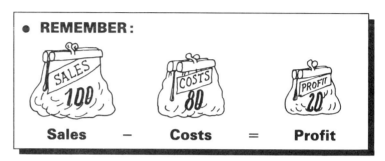

● **REMEMBER:**

Sales   **–**   **Costs**   **=**   **Profit**

Cut your costs by reducing your waste, and you will get a bigger profit.

Sales   **–**   **Lower costs**   **=**   **More profit**

CUTTING THE COST OF RAW MATERIALS

The cost of materials can be made less by–

● *Good buying.* This is even more important in manufacturing than in retail trade. Price is not everything. Cheap materials may mean more material that cannot be used because it is faulty and must be thrown away, so that the material you can use becomes dearer.

● *Cutting down waste.* In woodworking, sheet metalworking, shoemaking, dressmaking and tailoring, among other trades, skilled cutting can make great savings as against bad cutting.

● *Cutting down spoiled work.* This must then be thrown away or sold off cheaply. When work must be scrapped, you lose not only the cost of machine time but also the money which you would make if the product were sold.

BAD CUTTING GIVES ONE SHIRT BUT **GOOD CUTTING** GIVES TWO SHIRTS

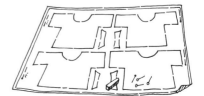

Good training of workers, good tools and working conditions, good wages and strong supervision will cut down spoiled work.

CUTTING LABOUR COSTS

This will not be done by cutting wages. It must be done by cutting down the amount of time which a worker wastes when he is doing a job. The costs of labour are calculated on the basis of the time spent by a worker to do a certain piece of work. The less the time spent, the less the cost.

How is time wasted by workers?

- By making workers walk, and carry materials through the workshop further than they need, because machines, workplaces and stores are badly placed.
- By giving workers bad workplaces, which are untidy, difficult to work at and badly lit, and by giving them unsuitable or worn-out tools for the job to be done.

TIME IS WASTED BY:
WALKING TOO MUCH
POOR WORKPLACES
BAD TOOLS

WORKSHOP LAYOUT

Workshop layout is the way in which machines, workbenches and storage places in a workshop are placed in relation to each other.

Good layout means that the product travels and is handled as little as possible between stages of manufacture, and that people walk as little as possible. Bad layout means that the product travels and is handled too much during its manufacture, and that people walk too much.

Bad layout costs you money because products take longer to make than they need to take. To get the same output, you need:

▲ **BAD WORKSHOP LAYOUT** COSTS YOU MONEY AND CUTS PROFITS

- more workers;
- more handling equipment;
- more space (bigger factory buildings).

All these things mean more costs.

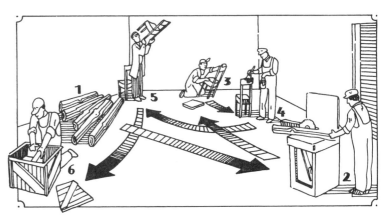

26

So your profits are less and you may lose orders to companies which do things better. It is *your* money you are wasting.

With bad layout, the product goes back and forward between processes. This uses more labour and more trucks, makes delays at machines and makes work difficult to find. Space is taken up in a bad way.

Good layout is most important when the product or materials used are heavy or big, as in sheet metalworking and woodworking. In wood machining the machines cut very fast. If the machines are in the right order there is little delay between the stages of manufacturing. The time spent moving big and heavy pieces of wood from the store to the shop, round the shop and on to the machines may be five or ten times as long as the cutting time.

If you are in a trade where heavy materials and work must be handled, think how you can make the handling time less.

You cannot always make the best layout, for example in an old factory building ; but one thing you can do is to *be tidy*.

- Keep your workshops tidy—put everything in its right place so that it is easy to find.

- Keep your gangways clear and tidy.

- Tidiness saves time and is safe.

▲ **GOOD WORKSHOP**
LAYOUT SAVES YOU MONEY AND INCREASES PROFITS

WORKPLACE LAYOUT

Workplace layout is the way in which tools and materials are laid out and the finished work is stored at the place where the work is done.

The workplace which you see in the picture on the left below can be seen in thousands of small workshops all over the world. What a mess!

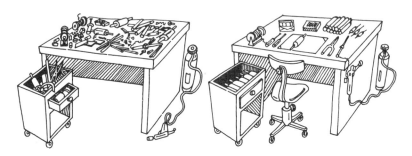

If you do not believe it, go and look at some small (and big) workshops near you. Finished work is mixed with pieces to be assembled. The tools are in the wrong places. The wire is tangled. The workers have to look for everything they want. They will take a much longer time to make one assembly than workers who sit at a neat workplace.

Now look at the picture on the right above. This is a good workplace layout. The worker has a chair to sit on, so he or she will be less tired. The pieces to be assembled are always in the same place so that they can be picked up without looking. The wire is on a reel. The welding nozzle is on a hook close to the worker's right hand. The screwdriver is hanging on a spring on the same side, easy to reach and use. The finished assemblies are put into a box on the left, ready to take away.

GOOD WORKPLACE LAYOUT MEANS EVERYTHING IN ITS RIGHT PLACE

Remember:

- **Good workplace layout is important where products are small and light and produced from many parts in large quantities.**

- **Work study will help you make better layouts and save money. Ask about it at your Small Business Centre or Management Centre.**

SAFETY

Workshop safety is extremely important both to you and your workers. As the owner/manager you are responsible for injuries and illness caused by poor safety standards or ignorance of risks that you and your workers are exposed to. Safety means not only preventing accidents but also doing something about bad working conditions like very loud noise or poor light, dangerous liquids or gases and so forth.

Remember that if something happens because you have not paid enough attention to workshop safety, you are causing other people pain and distress and you might end up paying for damages for the rest of your life.

There are a number of measures you can take in order to safeguard the health and security of your workers:

- Organise the work so that the different stages can be carried out smoothly and without pressure. Many accidents occur when people are moving in workshops from one workplace to another, or when they are collecting raw materials or carrying away finished goods.

- Give your workers detailed instructions on how to use machines, tools and chemicals before they start working. Make sure that the safety equipment that you provide is also used by your workers. Never let a worker without proper training repair or adjust machines.

- Avoid having visitors walking around in the workshop on their own. People who are unfamiliar with your business might not have the necessary respect for tools and machines.

- Always think about safety factors when you are making investments in new machines. Ask for written instructions on how to use them.

AVOID ACCIDENTS BY:

GOOD WORK ORGANISATION

TRAINING

SAFE MACHINERY AND EQUIPMENT

CUTTING THE COST OF MACHINES

CUTTING MACHINE TIME

Machines cost money, sometimes a lot of money. When you have paid money for a machine you must use it as well as possible. In many workshops, machines spend more time stopped than they do working. Why?

Because—

- the workers operating the machines must spend time fetching material from the store and taking away finished work;

- the next job is not ready when the earlier job is finished, and the worker and machine are waiting for work;

- the machines break down.

In addition to these causes, machines are often not working at their correct speeds, tools are not properly sharpened and the workers are not trained to use the machines well.

Before beginning work with a machine, make sure that it is working as well as possible and that the worker really knows how to use it well.

MACHINES COST MONEY–USE THEM WELL!

Let us look at an example of how time can be lost in working a machine during a working day of eight hours from 8 a.m. to 5 p.m. plus a one-hour meal break from 12.30 p.m. to 1.30 p.m.

Look at clock no. 1. The time during which the machine is producing work is shown in light grey. The time when the machine is stopped during the working day is shown in black. Clock no. 1. shows how you could operate your machine in the best way. There are no stoppages between 8 a.m. and 5 p.m. apart from the lunch break.

Clock no. 1

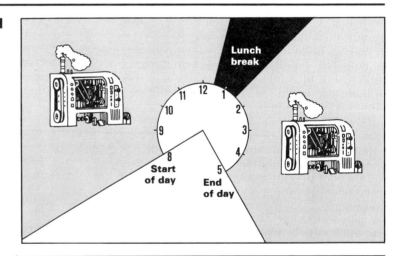

The machine worked for eight hours, with no stoppages.

Now look at clock no. 2 on the opposite page.

There are five dark grey pieces in clock no. 2.

Each dark grey piece shows the time when the machine was stopped, apart from at the lunch break, which is shown in black.

Clock no. 2

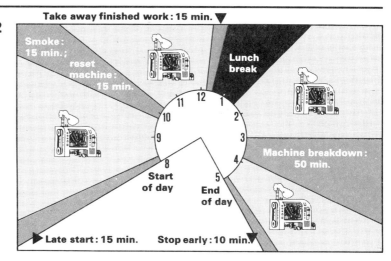

Clock no. 2 shows that you did not operate your machine in a good way. There were many stoppages for the following reasons:

● The worker is late	15 min. lost (8 a.m.-8.15 a.m.)
● The machine is reset	15 min. lost (9.45 a.m.-10.00 a.m.)
● The worker has a smoke	15 min. lost (10.00 a.m.-10.15 a.m.)
● The worker carries away finished goods	15 min. lost (12.15 p.m.-12.30 p.m.)
● The machine breaks down	50 min. lost (3.00 p.m.-3.50 p.m.)
● The worker stopped early	10 min. lost (4.50 p.m.-5.00 p.m.)
Total time machine stopped:	120 min. = 2 hr.

Due to the stoppages, the actual working time of the machine was reduced from eight hours to six hours, as below:

	Total working time of machine	8 hr. (480 min.)
Less:	Machine stopped	2 hr. (120 min.)
Gives:	Working time of machine	6 hr. (360 min.)

In other words, the machine was stopped for one-quarter (i.e. 25 per cent) of its total working time.

Now look at clock no. 3 on the next page and compare it with clock no. 2.

In clock no. 3 there is only one dark grey piece left.

Clock no. 3

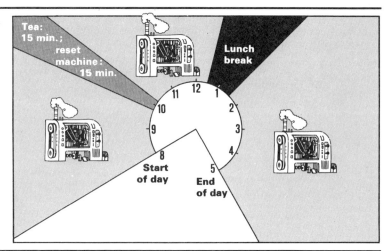

Let us see what has happened:

•	The worker starts on time	15 min. saved
•	The worker does not have to carry away finished goods	15 min. saved
•	The machine does not break down	50 min. saved
•	The worker does not stop work early	10 min. saved
	Total machine time saved:	90 min. = 1½ hr.

One-and-a-half hours of working time were saved due to management improvements. The actual working time of the machine was increased from six hours to seven-and-a-half hours, as shown below:

	Total working time of machine	8 hr. (480 min.)
Less:	Machine stopped	½ hr. (30 min.)
Gives:	Actual working time of machine	7½ hr. (450 min.)

In other words, the machine was stopped for only one-sixteenth (6 per cent) of its total working time.

MACHINE MAINTENANCE

Machine maintenance is looking after machines and equipment, including vehicles, by oiling, greasing, checking that they are in good working order, replacing worn parts before they break, and checking electrical parts and wiring.

To work well, maintenance must be done regularly: oiling and greasing, say, once a week; checking for worn parts once a month; and checking the electrical parts every three months. The more a machine costs, the more important is good maintenance.

REGULAR MAINTENANCE PREVENTS BREAKDOWNS

If you must stop a machine for a long time to do a good job on it, plan to stop it when you think it is best. It is better to stop a machine when you want to do it than to have it break down and stop when it is doing important work. By good maintenance, you avoid stoppages due to breakdowns.

HANDLING ON AND OFF MACHINES

We said earlier that in some trades it takes much longer to bring the material to the machine and to put it on the machine than it does to cut or work the material. It may also take longer to take the work off the machine. This is true of woodworking, where big logs of wood are difficult to handle. The same can be true of sheet metalworking, because the sheets are large and heavy. It can also be true of dressmaking when the dress or shirt is nearly finished.

HANDLING BY
HAND–**SLOW**

If you can only make the handling time in each operation smaller, you can make your output bigger. Many business people spend a lot of money on high-speed machines and lose most of the bigger output because they do not cut their handling time.

If you are in a trade where heavy materials and work must be handled, think how you can make the handling time less and get advice.

HANDLING BY
BARROW–**FAST**

CUTTING THE COST OF WORKING CAPITAL TIED UP

Cash is a most important asset used in running your business. Cash enables you to buy raw materials, pay your workers and office staff, and pay for all the other expenses such as rent, insurance, telephone and so on.

Cash flows into your business from five different sources:

- from your own savings;
- from loans which you obtain from a bank;
- from relatives or friends;
- from sales on credit; and
- from cash sales.

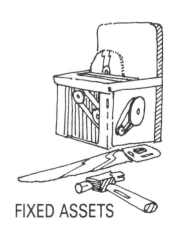

FIXED ASSETS

At the time you started your business, your cash came only from your own savings and maybe from a loan. You used this cash first of all to buy machines, tools, equipment and other assets. All these are called *fixed assets,* because they are fixed in your business for a very long time. This means that your money is tied up in them for a very long time.

WORKING CAPITAL

The rest of the cash, which you did not spend on fixed assets, is called *working capital.* You used it to buy raw materials and parts for production and to pay the wages and salaries and other expenses during the first two months or so of production. From then on you have received cash back from the finished goods which you make and sell.

You normally receive your cash in two ways:

- quickly when you make cash sales; and
- more slowly when you make sales on credit, since people take a long time to pay.

A CREDIT SALE
MEANS CASH LATER

A **CASH SALE**
MEANS CASH NOW

The cash which you receive from your sales is your new working capital. This is slightly more than the cash you spent on making the goods which you sold, because you made a profit. You now use this new working capital to buy more new materials and parts, which you convert into more finished goods and, when you sell these, this will give you even more cash (working capital) back than you spent before. Now you can see why this cash is called *working capital*: it *works* for you; it helps you to earn a *profit.*

WORKING CAPITAL
▼
BUYING MATERIALS
▼
MANUFACTURING OF GOODS
▼
SELLING OF GOODS
▼
MORE WORKING CAPITAL

Naturally, the faster you get your cash back after you spend it, the faster you make a profit and the faster your cash (working capital) increases. Therefore the raw materials which you purchased should be processed and turned into finished goods as quickly as possible, so that they can be sold and the money from sales flows back into your business.

It is very bad if your materials are held up in each section of your workshop for a long time. The more stock and material are lying in your workshop, the more working capital is tied up in them.

You should try to organise your production in such a way that you manufacture with a minimum of materials and semi-finished goods held up in your workshop.

Look at the example below, where a lot of working capital is tied up in stock in the workshop.

1. *Raw materials store*

   Working capital tied up in raw materials: 10,000

2. *Processing section*

   Working capital tied up in partly processed goods: 5,000

3. *Assembly section*

   Working capital tied up in partly assembled goods: 5,000

4. *Finishing section*

   Working capital tied up in partly finished goods: 2,500

5. *Inspection section*

   Working capital tied up in goods waiting for inspection: 2,500

6. *Finished goods store*

   Working capital tied up in finished goods lying in store: 5,000

   Total cash (working capital) *tied up in stock*: 30,000

Working capital tied up
10,000
+ 5,000
+ 5,000
+ 2,500
+ 2,500
+ 5,000
= 30,000

The more stock you hold, the more cash is tied up and the less cash you have in hand. Now look at the results you can obtain after making some improvements.

1. *Raw materials store*

   Working capital tied up in raw materials: 5,000

2. *Processing section*

   Working capital tied up in partly processed goods: 2,500

3. *Assembly section*

   Working capital tied up in partly assembled goods: 2,500

4. *Finishing section*

   Working capital tied up in partly finished goods: 1,250

5. *Inspection section*

   Working capital tied up in goods waiting for inspection: 1,250

6. *Finished goods store*

   Working capital tied up in finished goods lying in store: 2,500

   Total cash (working capital) *tied up in stock*: 15,000

Working capital tied up after improvements

5,000

+ **2,500**

+ **2,500**

+ **1,250**

+ **1,250**

+ **2,500**

= **15,000**

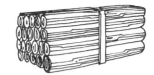

In the example above, you can reduce the money tied up in stock by moving the stock faster through the factory. You can do this in many ways. We have already talked about some improvements you can make:

- improved workshop layout;
- improved workplace layout;
- better machine maintenance;
- quicker loading and unloading of machines;
- shorter machine time.

You can also reduce the money tied up by:

- quick delivery of your finished goods to the customers after you have sold the goods, and

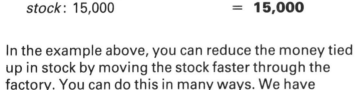

▲ REDUCE WORKING CAPITAL TIED UP BY:

HOLDING LESS STOCK

DELIVERING GOODS QUICKLY

LIMITING CREDIT SALES

getting as much of the payment in *ready cash* as quickly as possible;

- making sure that the customers to whom you sell on credit pay you cash strictly within two months after the delivery of the goods.

The saving in cash is: 30,000 − 15,000 = <u>15,000</u>. You now produce the same output with much less working capital tied up. With all this extra cash in hand, you may be able to finance all your purchases and expenses without having to go for a loan. You may even have some money to make the business bigger.

Increase your profit by using your working capital in a better way—Do not tie it up!

REMEMBER:
GOODS OUT **FAST**–
CASH IN **FAST**

SERVICE OPERATING

Service industries do not usually produce goods, but they render services to the public or some section of the public.

There are generally more small businesses in the service sector of industry than in the manufacturing sector. Service industries include garages and other repair workshops, television and radio repairs, laundries, dry-cleaning, passenger and goods transport services, hotels, restaurants and bars.

Business people in the service sector may think that the section of this book on manufacturing is of no use to them. It is true that some services, for example garages and repair workshops in general, and laundries, come very close to manufacturing industries, while others, such as bars, may seem very different. Although service industries do not generally use raw materials to make a product (although restaurants do), they use spare parts for repairs, fuel, heating, electricity and water for washing, cleaning, running vehicles and so on. They also use labour to repair, drive, clean, cook or serve, and equipment such as tools or vehicles, buildings and land just like manufacturing businesses.

To operate a service efficiently, we must use the same means as we use in manufacturing industry. The first step is to know your costs.

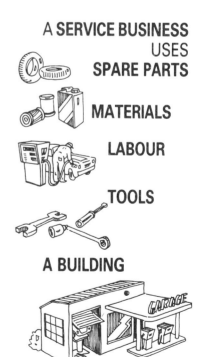

A **SERVICE BUSINESS**
USES
SPARE PARTS

MATERIALS

LABOUR

TOOLS

A BUILDING

JUST LIKE
A MANUFACTURING
BUSINESS

The same methods that are used in manufacturing to cut out waste and make sure of good use of workers' time and of machines can be used in operating services. Safety is also as important in a service industry as it is in manufacturing. Read the part of this section on "Manufacturing" carefully and see what you can apply in your service business.

KNOW YOUR COSTS

Knowing the costs of different items makes it possible to attack the biggest item of cost first. In manufacturing firms, this is generally the direct material cost but in service industries it may be direct labour, fuel or some other cost. To cut these costs you can use the same methods described for manufacturing:

ATTACK YOUR BIGGEST COST ITEM FIRST

- better buying and cutting down waste of materials, including fuel, power and energy;

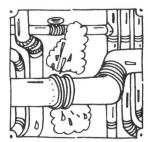 

CUT DOWN WASTE OF ENERGY

- reducing labour costs by better layout, working methods and tools, and by cutting ineffective time;

 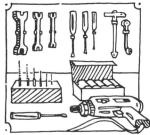

IMPROVE WORKPLACE LAYOUT

- improving the use of equipment, including vehicles, by better planning, including planned maintenance.

IMPROVE MAINTENANCE

BOOKKEEPING

3

Bookkeeping is writing down all the transactions arising from your business activities which can be expressed in money.

To run your business well you must know what money you have received, how much money you have spent and, most important of all, how you spent it. A bookkeeping system can provide you with that information. Good information removes the guesswork from business.

This section provides you with all the information you need to set up a simple, useful system of keeping records.

The books used for keeping records consist of a *ledger* and *subsidiary books.*

The ledger is the general book in which you enter almost all the figures arising from your business activities.

The subsidiary books are used to record information which will help you to remember important things about your business, e.g. the bills you have to pay or the wages you pay. The number of subsidiary books varies depending on the size and the kind of business you are in.

THE **LEDGER** IS THE MAIN BOOK

THE **SUBSIDIARY BOOKS** HELP YOU TO REMEMBER IMPORTANT THINGS

THE LEDGER

Every business transaction consists of two parts, one part that gives and one part that receives–one part that goes out of the business and in exchange one part that comes into the business. For example, if you sell goods, goods go *out* and cash comes *in*. Therefore you must make *two entries* for each business transaction.

If you sell goods, the goods go out of the business. Therefore you make an "Out" entry in the ledger. In place of what has gone out of the business, something else goes in. In this particular case money comes in for what is sold. You also make the "In" entry in the ledger.

A ledger consists of a number of *accounts.* An account is a column in the ledger that has been given a specific name, e.g. Cash, Bank, Sales and so on. In some ledgers a whole page is used as one account. Here we will use the type of ledger where a page is divided into several columns, each column regarded as one account.

CASH		BANK	
page1		page 2	

**One account
on each page**

CASH		BANK		SALES		RAW MAT.*	

**Several accounts
on each page**

* RAW MAT. = raw materials

STEP 1

The carpenter sells a chair to a customer. We need two accounts to record that transaction: one account to record the money that goes into the business (the Cash account) and one account to record the value of the chair that goes out of the business (the Sales account).

Our ledger now has two accounts, one called "Cash" and one called "Sales". The Cash account has three columns. One column is marked "In". This is used for

			CASH						SALES			
			In	Out	Bal.				In	Out		

entries when money comes into the business. The next column is marked "Out". This is used when money goes out of the business. The third column is for the Balance, or "Bal." for short.

Look at the Cash account below.

Suppose the carpenter gets 100 NU for the chair. Assume that there was 300 NU in the cash box before the sale of the chair. The entries step by step will be as follows:

CASH		
In	Out	Bal.
		300

CASH		
In	Out	Bal.
		300
100		

CASH		
In	Out	Bal.
		300
100		400

1 **Before the sale of the chair. The balance in the cash box is 300 NU**

2 **100 NU has gone into the business as a result of the sale of the chair**

3 **The addition of 100 NU to the 300 NU already in the cash box makes 400 NU**

The Cash account and the account showing what we have in our bank account are the only accounts where this "Balance" column is used. All other accounts are divided into two columns, one "In" and one "Out". The reason why there is a Balance column in the Cash and the Bank accounts is that we want to know instantly how much money is present in the business.

STEP 2

Let us enter the sale of the chair in the Sales account. The value of the chair was 100 NU and the chair has now gone out of the business. The entry of 100 NU will be made in the "Out" column of the Sales account, and 100 NU goes into the "In" column of the Cash account.

In the ledger below we have now entered all the figures arising from the sale of the chair.

SALES					CASH					SALES	
In	Out			In	Out	Bal.				In	Out
						300					
	100	▶		100		400					100

There are two accounts in the ledger. We must add more accounts, but first let us look at the space to the left of the Cash account. There we make some remarks concerning each transaction. We write the date of the sale and also write that it was a chair that was sold.

Finally, we shall give this transaction an identification number (Id.no.). We also write the number on the copy of the receipt we give to the customer. We keep the copy in a file together with other vouchers related to entries in the ledger.

KEEP ALL YOUR
VOUCHERS IN A FILE

Look at the columns to the left of the cash account below:

DATE	PARTICULARS	ID.NO.	CASH					SALES			
			In	Out	Bal.			In	Out		

The ledger entries are now added as shown below:

IN ▼   **OUT** ▼

DATE	PARTICULARS	ID.NO.	CASH					SALES			
			In	Out	Bal.			In	Out		
MAY					300						
2	1 CHAIR	86	100		400				100		

STEP 3

Let us add more accounts into our ledger.

OUT ▼   **IN** ▼

DATE	PARTICULARS	ID.NO.	CASH					SALES		RAW-MAT.	
			In	Out	Bal.			In	Out	In	Out
WAY					300						
2	1 CHAIR	86	100		400				100		
4	WOOD	87		150	250					150	

The carpenter has to buy raw materials. A Raw material account is needed. In the ledger above this account is added and we also have the following example entered: the carpenter buys wood and pays 150 NU cash to the supplier.

The ledger tells us that on 4 May wood was bought at a price of 150 NU. The cash was paid out, and after the payment 250 NU remains in the cash box. On the receipt given by the supplier of the wood the carpenter has written "87". The receipt can easily be found in the file where all the numbered vouchers are kept.

NUMBER ALL
YOUR VOUCHERS

STEP 4

We must pay wages to the workers. An account called "Wages" is added.

The carpenter pays four employees 50 NU each in cash, so 200 NU is taken from the cash box.

Look at the entry. Wages have been paid on 6 May. In total 200 NU is paid and the money is taken from the cash box (i.e. it is put into the "Out" column of the Cash account). We have 50 NU remaining in the cash box.

OUT ▽   IN ▼

	DATE	PARTICULARS	ID.NO.	CASH			BANK			SALES	
				In	Out	Bal.	In	Out	Bal.	In	Out
	MAY					300					
	2	1 CHAIR	86	100		400					100
	4	WOOD	87		150	250					
STEP 4 ▷	6	WAGES	88		200	50					
STEP 5 ▶	7	LOAN	89				6,000		6,000		

The reason why wages are entered in the "In" column of the Wages account is that the money represents the time the workers put into the business.

The vouchers in this case are the receipts signed by the workers when they receive their wages. The carpenter clips them together and notes "88" on them before filing.

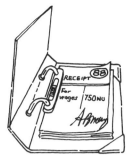

FILE YOUR WAGE RECEIPTS

STEP 5

The carpenter successfully applies for a loan at the local bank. The amount borrowed is 6,000 NU. He is requested by the bank manager to deposit the money in the bank until it is needed in the business.

In the ledger two new accounts are needed, one named "Bank" and one named "Loans".

The ledger now tells us that a loan was obtained on 7 May and that the money, 6,000 NU, was deposited in the bank. The document concerning the loan was given the identification number "89" and filed.

Remember that we said that every business transaction consisted of two parts: one part that goes

FILE YOUR DOCUMENTS

IN ▽				OUT ▼									
RAW MAT.		WAGES		LOANS		EQUIPMENT		INTEREST		DRAWINGS		OTHERS	
In	Out	In	Out	In	Out	In	Out	In	Out	In	Out	In	Out
150													
		200											
					6,000								

into the business and one part that goes *out* of the business. When this loan was obtained the money went *into* the account named "Bank". What went *out* of the business was a debit to the bank–a loan which has to be repaid. Therefore the entry in the Loan account will be in the Out column.

STEP 6

The money borrowed was meant to buy a drilling machine for the business. The price the carpenter had to pay was 4,000 NU. To record that purchase we have to add an Equipment account.

On 10 May a drilling machine was bought. The price was 4,000 NU and payment was made from the bank (i.e. by cheque). The receipt has the number "90" written on it and is kept in the voucher file.

STEP 7

To complete the carpenter's ledger we shall add just three more accounts. The first one we call "Interest". It is to be used when interest is to be paid on the loan which was obtained from the bank.

The second account we call "Drawings". It is to be used when the owner, the carpenter, withdraws

NOTE :

- EVERY TRANSACTION TAKES ONE WHOLE ROW ACROSS THE LEDGER

- NEVER ENTER MORE THAN ONE TRANSACTION ON EACH LINE

OUT
▽▼

	DATE	PARTICULARS	ID.NO.	CASH			BANK			SALES	
				In	Out	Bal.	In	Out	Bal.	In	Out
	MAY					300					
	2	I CHAIR	86	100		400					100
	4	WOOD	87		150	250					
	6	WAGES	88		200	50					
	7	LOAN	89				6,000		6,000		
STEP 6 ▷	10	DRILLING MACHINE	90					4,000	2,000		
STEP 7 ▶	13	INTEREST	91					200	1,800		
STEP 7 ▶	13	OWN SALARY	92					400	1,400		
STEP 7 ▶	15	ELECTRICITY	93					150	1,250		

money or goods from the business for his private use.

The last account we call "Others". This account is used only when none of the others can be used.

Look at the examples given as entries in each of the three accounts.

If you are ever in doubt whether to use the "In" or "Out" column for a particular entry, start by making the entry in the Cash or Bank account first. If it is an "In" entry in the Cash or Bank account, the other entry has to be an "Out" entry.

STEP 8

There are only three more things left to remember:

- When you are starting up your ledger you must enter some details about the assets and liabilities of your business.
- When one page is full you must add up the columns and carry the totals to the next page in the ledger. These are called "Balances forward" (B/f).
- At the end of each month you must summarise each account.

▲ **MAKE IT A RULE**

ALWAYS START BY MAKING THE ENTRY IN THE **CASH** OR **BANK** ACCOUNT FIRST

		IN ▽		IN ▼		IN ▼		IN ▼		IN ▼		IN ▼	
RAW MAT.		WAGES		LOANS		EQUIPMENT		INTEREST		DRAWINGS		OTHERS	
In	Out	In	Out	In	Out	In	Out	In	Out	In	Out	In	Out
50													
		200											
					6,000								
						4,000							
								200					
										400			
												150	

Entering assets and liabilities

You must enter figures for the following four items when you start to use the ledger. ▶
These entries are only made *once*:

If we assume that the carpenter had the following assets and liabilities to enter
when he started to use his ledger, the first row on the first page will look as shown ▶
opposite:

DATE	PARTICULARS	ID.NO.	CASH			BANK			SALES		RAW MAT.	
			In	Out	Bal.	In	Out	Bal.	In	Out	In	Out
▶ MAY		B/f			300			1,800				

Balances forward (B/f)

When a page is full of entries you must add up the columns and carry the balance
forward to the next page. This is easily done. Look at the example below. The first
illustration shows the bottom half of one page in the ledger and the second
illustration shows the upper half of the following page in the ledger with the
balances carried forward.

DATE	PARTICULARS	ID.NO.	In	Out	Bal.	In	Out	Bal.	In	Out	In	Out
20	2 SOFAS	116	2,000							2,000		
20	OWN SALARY	117		600								
22	TELEPHONE	118		400								
23	NAILS	119		60								60
24	6 CHAIRS	120	900							900		
		B/f	4,800	3,200	1,600	8,000	6,300	1,700		5,200	1,400	

DATE	PARTICULARS	ID.NO.	CASH			BANK			SALES		RAW MAT.	
			In	Out	Bal.	In	Out	Bal.	In	Out	In	Out
MAY		B/f	4,800	3,200	1,600	8,000	6,300	1,700		5,200	1,400	
24	GLUE	121		40	1,560						40	
25	1 CHAIR	122	100		1,660					100		
25	WAGES	123		400	1,260							
29	LOAN REPAYMENT	124					300	1,400				
31	WATER	125		60	1,200							

Assets/Liabilities	Entry	
Money in the cash box	Balance column	Cash account
Money saved in the bank	Balance column	Bank account
Value of machinery, tools, cash register, etc.	In column	Equipment account
Borrowed money in the business	Out column	Loan account

Money in the cash box	300
Money in the bank	1,800
Value of machinery and tools	9,000
Loan	6,000

WAGES		LOANS		EQUIPMENT		INTEREST		DRAWINGS		OTHERS	
In	Out	In	Out	In	Out	In	Out	In	Out	In	Out
			6,000	9,000							

SUMMARISE EACH COLUMN AND CARRY FORWARD THE TOTALS TO THE NEXT PAGE

								600			
									400		
600			6,000	9,000		200		1,000		800	

WAGES		LOANS		EQUIPMENT		INTEREST		DRAWINGS		OTHERS	
In	Out	In	Out	In	Out	In	Out	In	Out	In	Out
600			6,000	9,000		200		1,000		800	
400											
		300									
										60	

DATE	PARTICULARS	ID.NO.	CASH			BANK			SALES		RAW MAT.	
			In	Out	Bal.	In	Out	Bal.	In	Out	In	Out
MAY		B/f	4,800	3,200	1,600	8,000	6,300	1,700		5,200	1,400	
24	GLUE	121		40	1,560							40
25	1 CHAIR	122	100		1,660					100		
25	WAGES	123		400	1,260							
29	LOAN REPAYMENT	124					300	1,400				
31	WATER	125		60	1,200							
			4,900	3,700		8,000	6,600					
					1,200			1,400		5,300	1,440	

Summarising at the end of a month

At the end of a month you must add up each column and carry forward the balance of each account to a new page in the ledger. See how it is done in the example above.

As you can see, it is only the net balance on each account which we carry forward to the next month (i.e. the next page). On the Cash and Bank accounts it is very easy as we have noted the net balance after each entry. But look at the Loans account. An instalment payment of 300 NU was made and we have to subtract that figure from the loan to find out the net balance.

As you have seen on most of the accounts, only one column is used, either the "In" or the "Out" column.

DATE	PARTICULARS	ID.NO.	CASH			BANK			SALES		RAW MAT.	
			In	Out	Bal.	In	Out	Bal.	In	Out	In	Out
JUNE		B/f			1,200			1,400		5,300	1,440	
2	1 SOFA	126	1,000		2,200				1,000			
2	A NEW LEDGER	127		50	2,150							

WAGES		LOANS		EQUIPMENT		INTEREST		DRAWINGS		OTHERS	
In	Out	In	Out	In	Out	In	Out	In	Out	In	Out
600			6,000	9,000		200		1,000		800	
400											
		300									
										60	
		300	6,000								
1,000			5,700	9,000		200		1,000		860	

But occasionally the other column is used : for example, when a customer returns a commodity and gets his money back, then you have to use the "In" column of the Sales account. Finally, have a look at the page for the new month below, with the balances brought forward.

Now you have learned how to set up a ledger and how to conduct what is called *double-entry bookkeeping.*

We have used "In" and "Out" as headings for each account. Professional bookkeepers will instead of "In" use the word "Debit", and instead of "Out" use the word "Credit". When you have become familiar with making entries in *your* ledger, you can do what the professionals do and use "Debit" and "Credit".

IN EQUALS **DEBIT**

OUT EQUALS **CREDIT**

WAGES		LOANS		EQUIPMENT		INTEREST		DRAWINGS		OTHERS	
In	Out	In	Out	In	Out	In	Out	In	Out	In	Out
,000			5,700	9,000		200		1,000		860	
										50	

THE SUBSIDIARY BOOKS

A complete bookkeeping system consists of the ledger and a set of subsidiary books. The number of subsidiary books used depends on the size and kind of business you are in. These books help you to remember important things about your business. Here are some examples of subsidiary books and how to use them.

THE INVOICE BOOK

The invoice book helps you to remember who owes the business money for goods or services you have sold but have not been paid for. When you have delivered a commodity or provided a service, you send an invoice to the customer. You keep a copy of the invoice in the invoice book.

When the customer pays his debt, you enter the amount in the ledger, take the copy of the invoice from the invoice book, mark it "Paid" and file it in the voucher file.

If the customer only partly pays the invoice, the copy of the invoice remains in the invoice book until it is fully paid. Just note on the copy how much is paid. For each part-payment you give the customer a *receipt*. Enter what is paid in the ledger and put the copy of the receipt into the voucher file. When the customer makes the last part-payment you remove the invoice copy from the book and mark it "Paid". File it in the voucher file.

The customer receives the chair and an invoice

The customer pays half of the invoice amount and gets a receipt

The customer pays the other half of the invoice amount and gets a second receipt

Ready-to-use invoice books and a pad of receipts can be bought in any stationery shop.

THE PURCHASE JOURNAL

The purchase journal is used to write down details of goods and services bought on credit which are not yet paid for.

The invoice you receive from the supplier is kept in the purchase journal until it is fully paid. If you are making part-payments to the supplier, write into the journal how much you pay. Each time you pay, also enter the amount in the ledger. File the receipts you receive for each part-payment in the voucher file. When you make the last payment you also file the invoice in the voucher file.

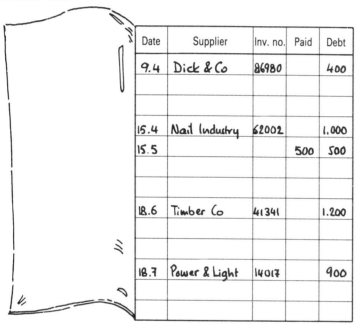

Date	Supplier	Inv. no.	Paid	Debt
9.4	Dick & Co	86980		400
15.4	Nail Industry	62002		1.000
15.5			500	500
18.6	Timber Co	41341		1.200
18.7	Power & Light	14017		900

Buy the journal in a stationery shop or use an exercise book and make the columns yourself.

THE WAGES BOOK

In this book you make notes about your employees: names, wages, advance payments and so on. Wages books can be bought from a stationery shop. When you pay your employees' wages, ask them to sign a receipt. Keep the receipts in the voucher file.

THE BUSINESS NOTEBOOK

Keep a separate book, a simple notebook for everything that happens between you and your business. Write down every sum of money you put into the business and everything you draw out, your salary and so on.

THE STOCK BOOK

The stock book is used to enter the figures arising from your stock-taking. Once or twice a year you must take stock. This means that you write down for each article the number of them you have, and also the value.

Stock-taking serves two main purposes:

● to see whether there are too many or too few articles in your stock;

● to be able to see if you have made a profit or loss during a certain period. Read more about this in the management accounting section of *Improve your business.*

A stock book can consist of sheets laid out as shown below or just an exercise book in which you write down the items.

Stock-taking List Date:			
Article	Qty.	Price	Total
Total stock value			

Stock-taking List Date: 30.6.86			
Article	Qty.	Price	Total
Wood 12x5cm	10m	10	100
Wood 10x5cm	20m	20	400
Glue	5ℓ.	60	300
Nails	8kg	25	200
Unfinished products			400
Chairs	8	100	800
Tables	3	200	600
Total stock value			2.800

THE INVENTORY BOOK

It is advisable to keep records of your machines and equipment in a book. The main purpose is to give you information you need for management accounting. The inventory book provides you with information about the present value of your machines and equipment. Each year you should subtract some money from the value because the equipment wears out. Subtract one-fifth of the value each year. After five years of use the value in your inventory book will be nil. This reduction in value each year is called "depreciation" (see the management accounting section of *Improve your business*).

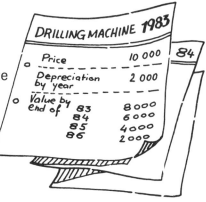

An inventory book can consist of sheets laid out as shown, or just an exercise book.

COSTING
AND PRICING

4

COSTING

Costing is the way you calculate how much each individual product or service costs you to produce and sell.

You need to know in detail what it costs to make a product, sell a product or provide a service. Many small and even large businesses get into trouble because they do not know their costs.

If you *know your costs*, you are able to:

● set your prices or give estimates and know if you are making a *profit*;

● find out which items are most *costly* in the running of your business, and if it is possible to reduce the costs;

● see what is the effect on your costs of any improvements you are planning and if your business can be more efficient.

▲ **KNOW YOUR COSTS**
AND YOU CAN:

SET PRICES

REDUCE COSTS

MAKE
IMPROVEMENTS

The information which you need for your costing comes from your bookkeeping system. You need documents such as payrolls, time-sheets and invoices. That is why your bookkeeping must be in good order before you can do your costing properly.

Before you calculate the cost of one product or one service job, you first have to know the *total* costs of running your business during one year. You also have to know the different types of costs which make up these total costs.

TYPES OF COSTS

In any business there are two types of costs:

● direct costs; and

● indirect costs.

Direct costs + indirect costs = total costs.

Direct costs are the costs of those items which become part of the products or services which you produce:

- raw materials and parts put into the product, known as *material costs;*
- wages and benefits (e.g. pensions, meal expenses) paid to the workers for the time they spend making the product, known as *labour costs.*

Indirect costs are the costs of all the other items which you need in running your business. They are also sometimes called *overheads* or *expenses:*

- the use of buildings, machines and equipment, their maintenance, repair and replacement;
- power, electricity and heating;
- salaries paid to everyone else not directly involved in making the product, including the owner's own salary;
- office costs (stationery, postage, telephone, etc.);
- selling costs other than salaries;
- financial costs (e.g. interest on your loan).

This basic breakdown of costs into direct and indirect applies to all types of businesses whether they are in retailing, wholesaling, manufacturing or providing a service (a garage, a restaurant, a lorry or a laundry). The only difference is that the raw material cost may be very small in some cases (e.g. a garage where the main cost is for the use of the labour of the mechanic).

When costing we sometimes talk about the *value added* to a product. Value added means the difference between the selling price and the total costs for one product.

Look at the following examples:

1. A manufacturer

   For a manufacturer, *direct costs* are the cost of raw materials and labour that go into the making of the products. Labour and raw materials are equal in amount and together they account for 80 per cent of total costs. The *indirect costs,* the office and transport to deliver the goods, account for 20 per cent of total costs.

DIRECT COSTS:

MATERIAL COSTS

LABOUR COSTS

INDIRECT COSTS:

BUILDINGS AND MACHINERY

POWER

SALARIES

OFFICE COSTS

SELLING COSTS

FINANCIAL COSTS

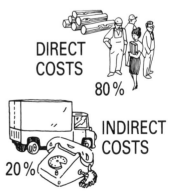

DIRECT COSTS 80%

INDIRECT COSTS 20%

TOTAL: 100%

2. A restaurant

For a service industry, *direct costs* are the costs of raw materials and labour that go directly into the services you give. In a restaurant the raw material costs are mostly food, while the labour costs are less than half the food. Direct costs account for 80 per cent of total costs. The *indirect costs,* heating, rent and other costs such as the services of waiters, account for 20 per cent of total costs.

DIRECT COSTS

55% 25%

INDIRECT COSTS 20%

TOTAL: 100%

3. A garage

A garage is also a service industry. The *direct costs* are mostly the cost of labour, while the raw materials (parts) are less than half the cost of the labour. Direct costs account for 85 per cent of total costs. The *indirect costs*, the office and the sales representative, account for 15 per cent of total costs.

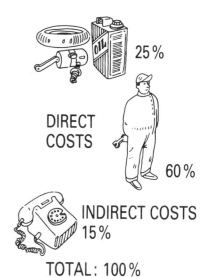

25%

DIRECT COSTS

60%

INDIRECT COSTS 15%

TOTAL: 100%

4. A shop

For a trader, *direct costs* are simply the amounts you pay to your suppliers for the goods which you bought from them, including the transport costs necessary to get the goods into your shop. *Indirect costs* are the costs of the shop rental, lighting, cleaning and decorating, the assistant's wages and so on.

DIRECT COSTS 80%

INDIRECT COSTS 20%

TOTAL: 100%

When you know the total costs of your business and the breakdown of the total costs into direct and indirect costs, you can work out the cost of an individual product or service.

COSTING ONE PRODUCT

The cost of making any article or operating any service is made up of several different cost items. Costing is so very important to every manufacturer that in this section we show you first how to calculate the cost of one product.

Let us start with an example of a carpenter who makes wooden tables. We will calculate the cost of making one wooden table.

The costs of making this table are divided into direct costs and indirect costs.

▲ DIRECT COSTS + INDIRECT COSTS = TOTAL COSTS OF ONE PRODUCT

HOW TO CALCULATE THE DIRECT COSTS

The direct costs are made up of two inputs: direct labour costs and direct raw material costs.

Direct labour costs

The direct labour costs for one table are easy to calculate.

1. *You take the monthly wage bill for the factory for the production workers and the supervisor*

   Suppose the carpenter has five production workers and one supervisor. The monthly wages of a worker including social benefits are 1,750 NU, while the monthly wages of the supervisor including social benefits are 3,000 NU. The total monthly wage bill is thus:

   5 workers × 1,750 NU   =   8,750 NU
   plus:
   1 supervisor × 3,000 NU =   3,000 NU
   Total monthly wage bill = 11,750 NU

2. *From the monthly wage bill, now calculate the total yearly wage bill*

   The total yearly wage bill for the carpenter is:
   11,750 NU × 12 months = 141,000 NU

3. *Calculate the total number of hours which will actually be worked during this year by the production workers*

   You can make an estimate of this by taking the figures from the accounts for last year.

TO CALCULATE THE **DIRECT LABOUR COSTS** OF ONE PRODUCT:

1 TAKE THE MONTHLY WAGE BILL FOR YOUR PRODUCTION WORKERS

2 CALCULATE THE YEARLY WAGE BILL

3 CALCULATE TOTAL HOURS WORKED

The total number of hours per year worked in the carpenter's workshop were:

47 weeks × 40 hr. × 5 workers = 9,400 hr.

4. *Calculate the hourly labour cost as follows*

$$\frac{\text{Total yearly wage bill}}{\text{Total number of hours worked in a year}}$$

For the carpenter:

$$\frac{141,000 \text{ NU}}{9,400 \text{ hr.}} = 15 \text{ NU per hr.}$$

4 CALCULATE THE HOURLY LABOUR COST

5. *Estimate the number of hours needed to make the table*

In the carpenter's workshop this is:

Labour time taken		No. of workers		Total no. of hours
4.7	×	2	=	9.4

5 ESTIMATE NUMBER OF HOURS NEEDED TO MAKE THE PRODUCT

6. *Now calculate the direct labour costs for the table*

For our carpenter:

Total no. of hours		Hourly labour rate		Direct labour cost per table
9.4	×	15 NU	=	141 NU

6 CALCULATE THE DIRECT LABOUR COSTS OF THE PRODUCT

Direct material costs

To calculate the direct material costs for one table, just add up the costs of all the materials and parts that are used in manufacturing. These costs must include the pieces wasted.

Total direct material costs for one table			
Item	Quantity	Cost	Cost per table
Top	10 m	15 per m	150
Frame	6 m	15 per m	90
Legs	4 m	10 per m	40
Glue	500 g	8 per kg	4
Paint	500 g	12 per kg	6
Total direct material costs per table:			290

▲ DIRECT MATERIAL COSTS ARE ALL THE MATERIALS USED IN MANUFACTURING

Total direct costs

The total direct costs for one table can now easily be calculated as follows:

Total direct labour costs for one table		Total direct material costs for one table		Total direct cost for one table
141 NU	+	290 NU	=	431 NU

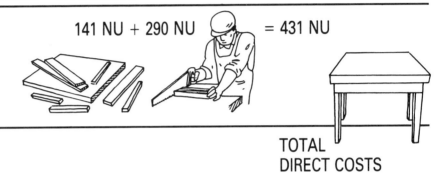

141 NU + 290 NU = 431 NU

TOTAL
DIRECT COSTS

HOW TO CALCULATE THE INDIRECT COSTS

Carpenters have many expenses other than the direct costs of making tables. They must repair their workshops; maintain and service the machines; run an office; pays interest on loans; sell the tables; and deliver them. These are the *indirect costs.*

Part of these indirect costs have to be included in the cost of each table. To calculate the indirect costs for one table, you first have to make an estimate of the total indirect costs for this year.

You can estimate the total indirect costs in your business by finding the figures for all the indirect cost items from your last year's accounts and adding them up. Add on a percentage which you think will cover the increase in prices which will result from inflation, e.g. 10 per cent or 20 per cent. In the example below we use a rate of 20 per cent inflation, but later on you will find examples where other rates of inflation are used.

If you do not have last year's figures available, write down each item of indirect costs and try to estimate how much you will spend on each of these items. Try to remember how much you spent on each item last year. If you do not know how to calculate your indirect costs, work through the Costing section of the *Workbook.*

Assume that the figures for indirect costs in the carpenter's workshop were as follows, and that 20 per cent was added to cover inflation:

▲ **INDIRECT COSTS**
ARE ALL THE COSTS OF BEING IN BUSINESS, SUCH AS:

- RENT
- INSURANCE
- POWER
- TELEPHONE
- MACHINE MAINTENANCE
- SALARIES
- SELLING COSTS
- INTEREST ON LOAN

Last year's figures	
Rent of building	12,000
Insurances of machines and stocks	2,000
Power and electricity	12,000
Telephone	3,400
Maintenance of machines	9,000
Salaries of office staff, cleaners and watchman	40,000
Selling costs	15,000
Interest on loan	5,000
Total indirect costs last year	98,400
+ 20 per cent of 98,400	19,600
= Total indirect costs this year	118,000

Once you have calculated an estimate for the total indirect cost, you can calculate the indirect cost per table. For a carpenter making only one product, like a table, this is very easy. The indirect cost per table is simply the total indirect cost divided by the estimated number of tables to be made during this year.

In this example the carpenter expects to make 1,000 tables:

$$\frac{1118,000 \text{ NU}}{1,000} = 118 \text{ NU}$$

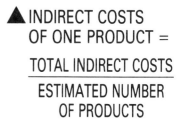

INDIRECT COSTS OF ONE PRODUCT =

$$\frac{\text{TOTAL INDIRECT COSTS}}{\text{ESTIMATED NUMBER OF PRODUCTS}}$$

HOW TO CALCULATE THE TOTAL COSTS

You can now calculate the total costs of making the table. This is shown below.

Total direct costs per table	431
+ Total indirect costs per table	118
= Total costs per table	549

We have calculated the cost of the table by supposing we shall make 1,000 tables. If the carpenter's sales for the year are very good and he sells 1,500 tables without increasing his indirect costs, then the indirect costs per table will be:

$$\frac{118,000}{1,500} = 79 \text{ NU}$$

The total costs of the table are now:

Direct costs per table	431
+ Indirect costs per table	79
= Total costs per table	510

TOTAL COSTS: 549 NU

TOTAL COSTS: 510 NU

MORE TABLES REDUCE COSTS PER TABLE

These costs are 39 NU less than when the carpenter made 1,000 tables. He can cut his selling price and still make a profit. By selling at a lower price he can have more customers.

When the carpenter makes fewer tables in the year without reducing the indirect costs, the cost per table goes up. If he has a bad year and sells only 500 tables, the indirect cost per table is:

$$\frac{118,000}{500} = 236 \text{ NU}$$

The total costs of one table are now:

	Direct costs per table	431
+	Indirect costs per table	236
=	Total costs per table	667

TOTAL COSTS: 667 NU

FEWER TABLES INCREASE COSTS PER TABLE

This is 118 NU more than when the carpenter made 1,000 tables.

His cost price (i.e. cost per table) is too high. If he wants to sell his tables and still make some profit on them, his selling price will probably be so high that his customers will not be willing to pay. They will buy from his competitors who sell at a lower price.

The more you can produce from the buildings, machines, offices and staff you have, the cheaper your product will be and the easier it will be to win business from your competitors.

COSTING MANY PRODUCTS

The simple example given above showed how the cost of a single product is built up from the different cost items. It can be used where only one product is made, like sacks of flour, fertiliser, cement building blocks, jute sacks and standard water pumps.

Very few small-scale manufacturers make one product only, because the market is generally not big enough.

A furniture-making firm will make tables of different sizes, chairs, beds, cupboards, school desks—whatever it can get orders for. The different products will take different quantities of material and different amounts of labour. The indirect costs cannot be divided in the way we have shown.

DIFFERENT PRODUCTS, DIFFERENT COSTS

HOW TO CALCULATE INDIRECT COSTS FOR DIFFERENT PRODUCTS

Assume that instead of making only tables, the carpenter makes also chairs and beds. He still employs five workers and one supervisor, and has the same amount of indirect costs for this year as in the above example.

An easy way of calculating the indirect costs for each product is to show them as a cost per hour of direct labour.

You do this as follows:

1. *Calculate the total number of hours which your employees in the workshop actually work during one year*

   You did this before.

   Remember the carpenter's example:

   > Total no. of hours worked in the year:
   > 47 weeks $\times$ 40 hr. $\times$ 5 workers = 9,400 hr.

2. *Divide the total indirect costs for this year by the total number of hours worked in a year*

   This gives you the indirect costs per hour worked.

   In our example:

   $$\frac{118,000 \text{ NU}}{9,400} = 12.55 \text{ NU}$$

Once you know this figure, it is very easy to calculate the indirect costs for each and every product, as follows:

1. *Calculate the total number of hours spent on making the product*

   For the table, this was two workers working for 4.7 hours = 9.4 hours.

2. *Calculate the total indirect costs of making one product by multiplying the number of hours spent by the indirect costs per hour calculated above*

   In the example above, the indirect costs for one table are:

   > 9.4 hours $\times$ 12.55 NU = 118 NU

TOTAL HOURS WORKED

47 $\times$ 40 $\times$ 5 workers = 9400 hr.

TOTAL INDIRECT COSTS

118,000 NU

TOTAL INDIRECT COSTS DIVIDED BY TOTAL HOURS WORKED GIVES **INDIRECT COSTS PER HOUR OF DIRECT LABOUR**:

$$\frac{118,000 \text{ NU}}{9,400} = 12.55 \text{ NU}$$

▲ TO CALCULATE THE **INDIRECT COSTS** OF EACH PRODUCT:

1 CALCULATE TOTAL NUMBER OF HOURS SPENT ON MAKING THE PRODUCT

2 MULTIPLY NUMBER OF HOURS BY INDIRECT COSTS PER HOUR

With this information you can calculate the total cost of making the product.

In the example of the table:

	Direct costs per table	431
+	Indirect costs per table	118
=	Total costs per table	549

You can calculate the costs of the other products in the same way:

THE CHAIR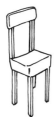

Direct material costs:		
4 legs of 1 m each @ 15 NU per m	60	
One seat ½ m × ½ m @ 24 NU per sq. m	6	
One back of ½ m × ½ m @ 24 NU per sq. m	6	72
Direct labour costs:		
One worker takes 6 hours 6 hours × 15 NU per hour		90
Total direct costs for one chair		162
Indirect costs:		
6 hours × 12.55		75
Total costs for each chair		237

THE BED

Direct material costs:		
Wood, total	460	
Nails, ½ kg @ 50 NU per kg	25	485
Direct labour costs:		
Three workers take 6 hours = 24 hours 24 hours × 15 NU		360
Total direct costs for one bed		845
Indirect costs:		
24 hours × 12.55		301
Total costs for each bed		1,146

PRICING

Pricing means deciding on the prices that you charge for your products or services.

In order to set prices you must know your costs. If you do not know your costs, you cannot know whether you are making a profit or a loss.

Many manufacturers, traders or service operators do not know their costs and think that they are less than they really are.

COSTING AND PRICING

Know your costs and you have a good basis for setting your prices. You can then compete with other manufacturers or operators and make a profit. Profit is needed to keep your business healthy. It will provide you with a reserve of money to see you through times when business is poor, to allow for unexpected events, to finance expansion or to repay loans.

Apart from knowing costs, there are many other factors that you have to take into account when setting your prices:

● What are the prices of your *competitors* for the same products or services, or for similar products or services which people could buy instead of yours?

● How much are your customers prepared to pay and how much *can* they pay?

● How does the price of a new product or service compare with the prices of the products or services that you are already selling?

You can sometimes tell when your pricing is wrong.

Prices may be too high if:

● you do not reach your sales target;

● you lose some big orders;

● sales of some of your products are low as compared to other products;

● stocks pile up;

● you receive complaints from customers.

▲ **PRICING**, DO IT **RIGHT**

WHEN **SETTING YOUR PRICES,** YOU MUST

● KNOW YOUR COSTS

● CHECK COMPETITORS' PRICES

● FIND OUT WHAT CUSTOMERS WILL PAY

● COMPARE PRICES OF NEW GOODS WITH THOSE OF EXISTING GOODS

HIGH PRICE: LOW SALES AND LOW PROFIT

Prices may be too low if:

- there are more orders than you can fill;
- you run out of stocks all the time;
- sales are good but overall profits are low.

LOW PRICE:
HIGH SALES BUT
LOW PROFIT

RIGHT PRICE:
SALES RIGHT AND
PROFITS RIGHT

PRICING FOR A MANUFACTURER

In the section on costing we showed how to calculate the costs of one table. These costs are used to set the selling price for the table.

Remember that the price you charge must cover:

- your direct costs;
- your indirect costs; and
- a reasonable profit.

Manufacturers will usually add between 20 per cent and 30 per cent on to their costs as profit. Sometimes the percentage added on is called the *mark-up*. Let us assume that the carpenter adds 30 per cent on to his total costs to arrive at his selling price as follows:

	Total costs per table	549
+	Profit = 30 per cent × 549 NU	165
=	Selling price	714

Note that the carpenter does not make 30 per cent profit on the sale. His profit on the sale is:

$$\frac{165\,\text{NU}}{714\,\text{NU}} \times 100 = 23 \text{ per cent on sales}$$

This is his *profit margin*. We shall come back to this point later in the chapter, in the section on mark-ups and margins.

▲ HOW TO PRICE

TOTAL
COSTS:
549 NU

NOW ADD
20 PER CENT PROFIT

The price that we just calculated is the price at which the carpenter *wants* to sell his product; but it might not be the price he can *get*. This depends on what is actually happening in the market.

- If tables of similar quality are selling at between 730 NU and 780 NU, he is in a good position. He can even raise his price to between 730 and 750 NU and be sure of selling his tables at a good profit.

- If tables of similar quality are selling at prices between 680 NU and 730 NU, he is still not in trouble. The price of 714 NU which he calculated is about right. His tables will sell with a bit of active marketing.

- But if the market prices are between 580 NU and 680 NU he finds himself in trouble. He will have to lower his price in order to sell. If he is unable to sell his tables for more than 580 NU, he seriously has to try to lower his costs. Although he still makes a profit of 31 NU on each table, this is not enough to keep his business healthy.

In many industries where you know that competition is severe, you cannot add 30 per cent for profit. You might try adding 20 per cent to your costs and see if your product sells. If you know your costs, you know what you are doing.

▲ACTIVE MARKETING
HELPS TO SELL

PRICING FOR A TRADER

For the trader, pricing is more important than costing. The prices you charge determine the quantity you will sell and therefore how much money will come into your business.

The money which comes in from sales must do three things:

- cover the *direct costs,* i.e. the cost prices of all the goods, including transport costs;

- cover the *indirect costs,* i.e. the costs of running the shop such as wages, rent, insurance, electricity and telephone; and

- provide a reasonable *profit.*

When fixing the selling price of an individual article, you must remember that the money you receive from the sale of that article still has to do these three things.

MONEY IN
FROM SALES

LESS
NEW STOCK

LESS
RUNNING COSTS
OF SHOP

GIVES
PROFIT

If you buy a packet of tea for 4.50 NU and sell it at 4.50 NU you collect enough to buy a new packet of tea—but you will not have any money to cover the costs of running the shop. You will not make any profit.

Retailers have to add a little to the prices of the goods they buy before they sell them to customers. This is called adding a *mark-up* to the goods. By doing this they will collect some extra money which will go towards the other costs, i.e. the costs of running the shop and some profit.

HOW TO PRICE

COST PRICE: 4.50 NU

+MARK-UP:
11 PER CENT

SELLING PRICE: 5 NU

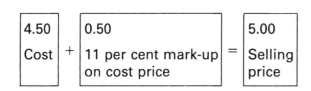

4.50		0.50		5.00
Cost	+	11 per cent mark-up on cost price	=	Selling price

Trade margins

All retail business owners add a mark-up in order to make a profit. In other words, they need a trade margin to cover their costs.

This trade margin is usually stated as a percentage of the selling price. In our example, the retailer has decided that she wants a trade margin of 10 per cent on the tea:

$$\frac{0.50}{5.00} \times 100 = 10 \text{ per cent}$$

Note: In order to obtain a *trade margin of 10 per cent* on the selling price of tea, she has to add *a mark-up of 11 per cent* on to the cost price of the tea. You will read more about this later.

The question for the retailer is how high the margins on her different goods should be. How do you know that the margins on your products are high enough to cover your indirect costs and in addition give you profit?

To answer this question, first look at the last year's results for your business. Make a summary of your sales and costs over the last year as follows:

Example: Trading of grocer's shop during 1984

	Sales	480,000
+	Direct costs	408,000
=	Gross profit	72,000
+	Indirect costs	52,000
=	Net profit	20,000

From this summary you can calculate your average trade margin as follows:

$$\frac{\text{Sales} - \text{Direct costs}}{\text{Sales}} \times 100 = \text{Average trade margin}$$

$$\frac{480,000 - 408,000}{480,000} \times 100 = 15 \text{ per cent average trade margin}$$

If you think this margin gives you enough profit you can try the same margin again during the coming year. But ask yourself if you are able to achieve this margin in your business. Look back at last year's results. Try to think whether you will be able to obtain the same margin again or if the margin can be higher.

If you are not satisfied with last year's results, you should then try to aim at a higher margin for the next year. You can do two things to achieve this:

● increase your prices; or
● decrease your costs.

Once you have decided on your average margin, you should then try to *achieve* it. This is not easy, because you will not be able to get the average margin on all your goods. On some goods you will be able to get higher margins than the average, while on others you will not be able to get as much as the average.

Try to fix the margins on your different goods in such a way that your total sales will give you approximately your average trade margin. There is no easy way to

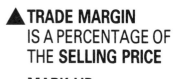

TRADE MARGIN
IS A PERCENTAGE OF THE **SELLING PRICE**

MARK-UP
IS A PERCENTAGE OF THE **COST PRICE**

INCREASE YOUR MARGIN BY **INCREASING YOUR PRICES**

OR **DECREASING YOUR COSTS**

ensure that you will eventually achieve your estimated average margin. Your business ability can guide you.

After six months make another summary of your trading and find out if your average trade margin was too low. If you think so, you can consider buying more of the luxury-type goods on which you can charge a higher trade margin. Maybe you can increase the margins on some of the goods that you already sell.

If your average trade margin was the same or even higher than your estimate but your sales were low, you might try to lower the margins on some of your goods in order to increase sales.

MARK-UPS AND MARGINS

Once you have decided on the margins for your different goods, you must now ask yourself the following question: By how much should I *mark up* the cost price of the product to get the *margin* which I want when I sell the product?

We have already seen an example of this: A retailer added a mark-up of 11 per cent on the cost price of her tea to get a trade margin of 10 per cent on its selling price.

The question is now: How does the retailer know that an 11 per cent mark-up will give her a 10 per cent margin?

It is possible to calculate the different mark-ups for each and every margin, but this is a difficult exercise. Therefore we have made things easier by giving you a chart on the next page, in which you can find the mark-up for each margin from 1 per cent to 50 per cent. The margins are given in the first column, the corresponding mark-ups in the second column. For example, a margin of 26 per cent corresponds to a mark-up of 35 per cent, and a margin of 12 per cent corresponds to a mark-up of 13.5 per cent.

Example

The grocer's shop has decided to sell its tea with a margin of 17 per cent. The cost price of one packet of tea is 3 NU. Look at the chart. The *mark-up* corresponding to a margin of 17 per cent is 20 per cent. We can now calculate the selling price of the packet of tea as follows:

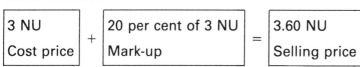

| 3 NU Cost price | + | 20 per cent of 3 NU Mark-up | = | 3.60 NU Selling price |

HIGH-MARGIN PRODUCTS

SOME HIGH, SOME LOW–TOGETHER THEY GIVE YOU THE **AVERAGE**

LOW-MARGIN PRODUCTS

HOW TO CALCULATE THE **SELLING PRICE** OF A PRODUCT:

1 DECIDE ON ITS **MARGIN**: 17 PER CENT

2 FIND THE **MARK-UP** FROM THE CHART ON THE NEXT PAGE: 20 PER CENT

3 ADD THE **MARK-UP** TO THE **COST PRICE** TO GET THE SELLING PRICE 3 NU + 20 PER CENT = 3.60 NU

Whenever you want to calculate the selling price of a
product, you can do so if:

- you know its cost price; and
- you have decided on its margin.

HANDY MARGIN CHART

MARGIN	MARK-UP	MARGIN	MARK-UP	MARGIN	MARK-UP
1	1.01	18	22.0	35	54.0
2	2.05	19	23.5	36	56.5
3	3.1	20	25.0	37	59.0
4	4.2	21	26.5	38	61.5
5	5.3	22	28.0	39	64.0
6	6.4	23	30.0	40	66.5
7	7.5	24	31.5	41	69.5
8	8.6	25	33.5	42	72.5
9	10.0	26	35.0	43	75.5
10	11.0	27	37.0	44	78.5
11	12.5	28	39.0	45	81.5
12	13.5	29	41.0	46	85.0
13	15.0	30	43.0	47	88.5
14	16.5	31	45.0	48	92.5
15	17.5	32	47.0	49	96.0
16	19.0	33	49.5	50	100.0
17	20.5	34	51.5		

PRICING FOR A SERVICE OPERATOR

Service businesses such as restaurants, garages, dry cleaners, travel agencies or transport operators do not produce or sell products that you can see or touch. They offer people a service in exchange for money. This can be through the use of a machine (dry cleaning) or the work of a skilled worker (a mechanic in a garage).

In service businesses *direct costs* are the costs of using that machine or that worker.

Indirect costs are all the other costs that you have to pay for running the business, e.g. rent, administration expenses, office costs, insurance, telephone and so on.

The money that you get for your services should be high enough to cover:

- the direct costs;
- the indirect costs; and
- a reasonable profit.

The price for a service is usually calculated on an hourly basis. This is called the *rate per service hour.* It is built up as follows:

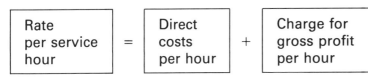

| Rate per service hour | = | Direct costs per hour | + | Charge for gross profit per hour |

The charge for gross profit per hour is added to cover the indirect costs plus a profit.

EXAMPLE

The rate per service hour for the Good Service Garage would be as follows.

Direct costs per service hour

The direct costs per hour are easy to calculate. In the Good Service Garage, the direct costs are the wages (including social benefits) of the workers. You can calculate the labour cost per hour as follows:

1. Estimate the total number of hours for which your workers will get paid during the next year. The easiest way to do this is to look at the past year's

REPLACEMENT OF TYRE: 10 NU

COVERS DIRECT COSTS, INDIRECT COSTS AND A PROFIT

HOW TO CALCULATE YOUR DIRECT COSTS PER SERVICE HOUR

1 ESTIMATE THE NUMBER OF HOURS TO BE WORKED NEXT YEAR

figures. Last year, Good Service employed five workers. The total number of paid hours in the past year was:

| 5 workers | × | 40 hours a week | × | 47 weeks a year | = | 9,400 hours |

Good Service estimates that the total number of paid hours for next year will be the same as in the past year.

2. Estimate the total wage bill for the next year by looking into your wages book for the past year.

The total monthly wages, including benefits, in Good Service were:

Five workers × 1,000 NU	=	5,000
+ One supervisor × 1,500 NU	=	1,500
= Total monthly wage bill		6,500
Total yearly wage bill is 6,500 NU months × 12	=	78,000 NU

From the above you estimate your next year's total wage bill. Let us assume that the total wage bill for next year will be the same as the figure for the past year.

3. Divide the total wage bill for next year by the total number of hours to be worked next year (9,400 hours). This gives you the direct costs per hour:

$$\frac{78,000\,NU}{9,400} = 8.30\,NU \text{ per hour}$$

Charge for gross profit per service hour

To determine the hourly gross profit charge, it is necessary that you know:

- how much your total indirect costs will be for the next year;

- how much net profit you want to make in your business.

The easiest way to get some ideas about this is to make an estimate of your sales and costs for the coming year.

Good Service's sales and costs estimates for next year are:

	Revenues from repairs	270,000
−	Direct costs (wages)	78,000
=	Gross profit	192,000
−	Indirect costs	172,000
=	Net profit	20,000

To obtain the amount of gross profit it is necessary to recover a part of it during each hour worked. The hourly charge for recovery of gross profit is thus:

$$\frac{\text{Gross profit next year}}{\text{Total hours to be worked in the next year}} = \text{Hourly charge for gross profit}$$

For Good Service this is:

$$\frac{192,000\,\text{NU}}{9,400} = 20\,\text{NU}$$

We can now calculate the *rate per service hour* by adding up the direct costs per hour and the charge for gross profit per hour as follows:

	Direct costs (labour) per service hour	8.30
+	Charge for gross profit per service hour	20
=	Total rate per service hour for next year	28.30

HOW TO CALCULATE YOUR HOURLY CHARGE FOR GROSS PROFIT
▼

ESTIMATE YOUR GROSS PROFIT FOR THE NEXT YEAR
▼

DIVIDE THIS BY THE TOTAL NUMBER OF HOURS TO BE WORKED NEXT YEAR

NOTE TO COSTING AND PRICING

We suggest that in all the examples of this section you take note of the following idea and try to apply it in your calculations.

In all our calculations we assumed that the workers are actually employed on work during the whole of their paid working hours. Unfortunately, in a real-life situation, this is rarely true. At times, you may have no work for your workers to do because you have no orders.

There will also be times when they may sit around or waste time before they start the next job. Out of every

100 *paid* working hours you will probably only be able to *employ* your workers on actual work for 70 or 80 hours. This affects your calculations of direct labour costs and indirect costs per hour.

A simple way in which you can allow for this in your calculations is to multiply your estimate of the total number of hours worked by a factor which you think, from your experience, corresponds to the actual percentage of work which your workers do for you. For example, if you estimate that your workers actually work for 70 hours out of every 100 paid working hours, then the factor will be 0.7 (70 per cent).

In the example of the garage given above, you should multiply as follows:

$$9,400 \text{ hours} \times 0.7 = 6,580 \text{ hr.}$$

Note that if you use this figure, it will give you a higher rate for the direct labour costs per hour and the indirect costs per hour. These rates are more correct but note that they are *higher*.

AT TIMES THERE IS NO WORK

If you adopt this idea and apply the method, it will mean that the prices you charge for your products must, in turn, be higher if you want to get back enough money to pay for the times where there is just no work being done.

MARKETING

5

Marketing is getting people to want your goods, selling them, delivering them to the buyers and getting paid for them.

Marketing means being active in every way which will help to increase sales. It is not enough to sit and wait for orders.

This is what you have to do:

● find out what customers want;

next:

● choose the products or services you can offer to satisfy their wants;

● price and sell them;

● promote and advertise them;

● place them in the market and distribute them;

and:

● make a profit at the end of the whole process.

▲ FIND OUT WHAT THE CUSTOMERS WANT

PRODUCE, PRICE, PROMOTE AND PLACE THE PRODUCT

MAKE A PROFIT

CHOOSING THE GOODS TO BE MADE AND SOLD

Choosing the goods to be made and sold means:

● **deciding on the designs;**

● **deciding on the quality;**

● **deciding on the quantities you think you can sell.**

People like something a little different from what their friends have—but not too different! People change their ideas slowly and like things which they know and have grown up with. If you make something too different, only a few people will buy it.

Think about the product you are going to make and sell. Try to imagine what the customers would like the product to be.

FINDING OUT WHAT CUSTOMERS WANT

In the section on "Buying and selling" we said that business people must know their customers. They must find the right answers to many questions such as:

- Whom am I trying to sell to?

- What kind of designs, colours, sizes and so on do they like?

- Where are the customers—in the capital city, in the provinces, in smaller towns or in the country?

- When do they buy—all the year round, in winter, in summer, at holiday times?

- How many do they want, can they afford them and can I sell them?

Finding the answers to these questions and others is called *market research.* You may find out many facts from:

WHAT KIND OF PRODUCT DO MY CUSTOMERS WANT?

- WHICH DESIGNS?
- WHICH PRICES?
- WHICH SIZES?
- WHICH QUALITY?

1 Your own order books

2 Your sales representatives

3 Wholesalers and retailers you sell to

4 Customers who use your goods

5 Other manufacturers' catalogues

6 The Chamber of Commerce

FEW OR MANY DIFFERENT GOODS?

One mistake some manufacturers make is to try to sell to everyone. They make too many different sorts of goods, or too many sizes or models of the same goods. It is sometimes difficult to decide what to make. If you are a tailor, should you make only men's white shirts, which you do very well, or should you make sports shirts or women's blouses or dresses...?

The more different goods or models you make, the more your customers have to choose from *but* the more it will cost you to make each article. This is because you will buy your different materials in smaller quantities; this will cost more and you will not be able to organise your production so well. Your competitors who make only one or two goods in large quantities can sell cheaper than you can.

If you are sure your product is good but it does not sell well, you should put more effort into your marketing. Do not try to make more different items but try to sell what you already make!

WIDE CHOICE—
HIGH
PRODUCTION COST

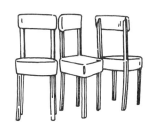

LESS CHOICE—
LOW
PRODUCTION COST

PROMOTION AND ADVERTISING

Promotion includes every way you influence people so that they will buy your goods.

Advertising is telling people what you have to sell so that they want to buy your goods more than they do those of your competitors.

What you are selling, whom you are selling to and where customers live will decide what sort of advertising you use and what media you use. Media in advertising are the means used to tell people about your goods, except word of mouth.

Media include newspapers, magazines, radio, television, cinemas and posters.

If your goods are sold to very many people throughout the whole country you can use radio, local newspapers, signboards on main roads, posters on buildings, or even television if you can afford it and your sales are big enough.

Industrial and trade customers are special. They use your goods to earn their living. They want to know how

MEDIA YOU CAN USE
TO ADVERTISE
YOUR GOODS

your goods will help their businesses and they want hard facts, not promises. To reach them you must advertise in trade journals and through well-prepared catalogues.

Where you want to promote your products to a few special customers, send special letters to each one personally. At the beginning of a new year you could even send calendars, diaries, pencils or notepads as gifts with the name of your business printed on them.

The owners of businesses, bankers and top managers will read personal letters while they throw away a circular letter. Make sure your letters are on the best kind of paper with an impressive letter-head and very well typed. If your typist is not good enough to do this, use a typing agency. This is the way to promote a good image of your business.

Retailers can display promotional material in their shops, on the counter and in the window. This is called point-of-sale advertising. It may be a cut-out cardboard figure or an eye-catching poster showing particular goods.

Ask new customers how they first heard of your product or service. You will then get a good idea of how well your name is known and how your business is thought of in the market.

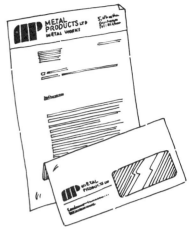

A BUSINESS LETTER NEEDS:

- A NEAT HEADING
- CLEAR INFORMATION
- GOOD TYPING

DISTRIBUTING

Distributing means getting goods from the manufacturers to the final customers. It includes buying and reselling goods by wholesalers and retailers and the transport used to move them at each stage.

How you sell and distribute your products depends on:

- what the products are;
- who the customers are;
- where the customers are;
- how many customers or people you hope to sell to;
- how much they buy.

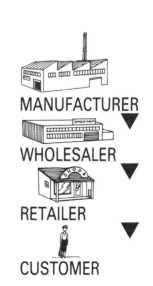

MANUFACTURER ▼

WHOLESALER ▼

RETAILER ▼

CUSTOMER

This can be seen very clearly in the table below.

What	Who	Where	Point of sale	Number of points	Sold by
Cheap clothes	Poorer people	Whole country	Stores, shops, markets, etc.	Very many	Salesmen, owner to big store buyers
Dear leather goods	Wealthy people, tourists	Capital city, tourist towns	Department stores, hotels, boutiques	Very few	Direct by owner
Chocolates and sweets	Everyone, especially children	Mostly towns	Shops, markets, street sellers	Very many	Salesmen, wholesalers, retailers
Kitchenware	Middle-income households	Mostly towns	Department and hardware stores	Not so many	Salesmen, owner (big orders)
Metal windows	Builders	Mostly big towns	Whole-salers, builders	Not so many	Owner, salesman, catalogue
Special tools and dies	Engineering and plastic industry, etc.	Capital, few big towns	Manufac-turer's factory	Very few	Owner, technical staff
Standard tables and chairs	Government, schools, institutes	Mostly big towns	Buyer's office, government or local officials	Very few	Owner

You can see that there are different ways and places for selling goods. If you are selling to the Government, you will have to go through the usual procedures. In some countries, goods for the general public go from the manufacturer to a wholesaler, to another wholesaler, and then in smaller lots to retailers or market sellers.

Four or five lots of people may handle the goods, each taking a profit, before they reach the buyer if he or she lives in the country. This puts up the price of the goods to the people who want them. You will sell fewer goods this way. You must find the best sales channels for your goods.

DECIDING HOW TO DISTRIBUTE YOUR GOODS

Very few small manufacturers can employ many sales representatives to visit customers, if they are selling all over the country.

Wholesalers can do the job for you by buying bigger quantities of goods and breaking them down into smaller lots to sell to retailers or to other customers. They can do the selling for you.

Wholesalers sell many different goods and may also sell the goods of your competitors. They will not always push your goods as hard as your own sales representatives do and they will only buy at a cut price, i.e. with a discount.

1

Manu-facturer

Wholesaler

Retailer

User

LONG CHANNEL

2

MEDIUM CHANNEL

3

SHORT CHANNEL

▲ DIFFERENT WAYS OF DISTRIBUTION

Wholesalers must not only make a profit to cover their costs but they must, if they are selling to retailers, allow them discount in order that they should have a profit.

If you sell to retailers you may make more profit but, if there are many retailers in different parts of the country, you may have problems of visiting them and of transporting the goods to them. Selling direct to retailers, if there are many, means that you must employ one or more sales representatives, even if you do some selling yourself.

In deciding what is the best means to use to sell and distribute your goods, you have to think about:

1. *The cost of selling* – will the cost of sales representatives' salaries and expenses be recovered by higher selling prices than a wholesaler might give you?

2. *Selling the goods* – will sales representatives push your goods better than a wholesaler will? Can they sell enough – more than a wholesaler – to cover their costs and make a bigger profit?

Cost price

Manufac-turer's selling price

Whole-saler's selling price

Retailer's selling price

▲ THE LONGER THE CHANNEL, THE HIGHER THE SELLING PRICE

3. *Storage* – goods for sale in distant parts of the country may be stored locally. Is it better to use a wholesaler or set up your own store in the region?

4. *Delivery* – to deliver goods to other regions, is it better to have your own transport, hire lorries, use a common carrier or, for small parcels, use the mail?

COMPARE SELLING THROUGH YOUR OWN SALES REPRESENTATIVES OR THROUGH A WHOLESALER

1 WHAT IS THE COST OF EACH?
2 HOW WELL DOES EACH PROMOTE YOUR PRODUCT?
3 HOW WIDELY CAN EACH COVER THE COUNTRY?
4 HOW QUICK IS EACH FOR DELIVERY OF YOUR PRODUCT?

MANAGING SALES REPRESENTATIVES

All the people in the business, including you, are sales representatives for the business.

The letters you write, the way they are typed, the way the telephone is answered, how quickly you answer letters, what you do about complaints – these add up to giving people outside (people who may buy from you) a picture of a well-run business with a good owner and staff or a poorly run business with a bad owner and staff.

The sales representatives you employ to sell your goods also give people an idea about the kind of business you have. Selling can be a lonely and tiring job. Sales representatives' time may be wasted by people who do not keep appointments. Customers may even go out without leaving a message or keep

MAKE YOUR CHOICE

▲ YOUR SALES PEOPLE ARE YOUR BUSINESS REPRESENTATIVES

them waiting for an hour or more. Some people do not think they must be polite to salespeople and are very rude. Yet sales representatives must be well dressed, polite and patient, they must never lose their temper and they must know about the goods they are trying to sell. They are ambassadors for the business and the company will be judged by how they act.

Sales representatives must fit in with the sort of customers they visit. It is no good sending a rough person, however good at his work, to visit educated people. However, sales representatives visiting artisans and small traders must be simple people, able to talk to them in their own words. They must also know the jobs which the small traders do and how to use the product they are selling.

Train your sales representatives in your products, especially if they are technical (machines, tools, electrical goods, fertilisers, medicines and so on). Make sure that they have the education and technical knowledge to be able to talk to technical people. Many small manufacturers, farmers, builders and other people using technical products come to trust a sales representative who can give them good advice, not only on the goods he is selling, but about their businesses. They will see him or her when they will not see other representatives and they will buy the goods – *your* goods.

One important way in which you can help your sales representatives – and win more orders – is to make sure that all letters, enquiries, reports and complaints from customers are dealt with at once.

If there is an enquiry or a complaint which you cannot answer at once, because you must study it or get more information, send a letter or even a postcard saying that you have received it and will reply as soon as you have the information.

Remember – your sales representative is the person who has to go back and see the customer, and the customer will be angry with him or her if you do not reply. Quick replies and politeness will build your representative up and build your business up in the eyes of customers.

▲ KNOWLEDGE OF YOUR PRODUCT HELPS YOUR SALES REPRESENTATIVE TO SELL

SALES RECORDS

Good sales records are very important. The more different goods or products you sell, the more important sales records are.

From good sales records you can find out:

- whether your sales are rising, falling or about the same from month to month or year to year;

- which goods or products are selling well, which are selling badly, which have sales that are going up or going down;

- in what regions the sales are best, worst or merely average;

- which designs or models customers like best;

- how your sales representatives are doing;

- how new products are selling;

- if older products are losing sales.

By having this information easily to hand you can watch your sales. If you see sales going down, you must find out why.

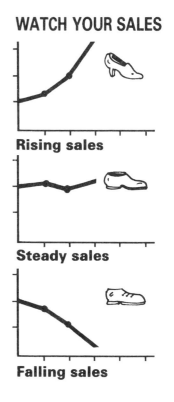

WATCH YOUR SALES

Rising sales

Steady sales

Falling sales

REASONS FOR FALLING SALES

This can be due to different causes:

- one of your competitors may be making a special drive for sales;

- your products may be going out of date;

- you may have a bad sales representative;

- customers may be unhappy with your quality (too many faulty goods), your deliveries (late, not in the right quantities) or your service.

Often when manufacturers make many different sorts or models of products, only 10 per cent of them sell well and make a profit. The other 90 per cent make little profit and may even make losses.

Good sales records make it possible to see changes in sales, to find out why they are happening and, if they are bad, to do something to make them better before it is too late.

IF THIS HAPPENS TO YOU—

FIND OUT **WHY** AND **DO** SOMETHING ABOUT IT

Good accounts mean that you can see what sales figures mean in terms of money, so that you can see on which products you are making a profit and on which a loss.

PAYMENT AND CREDIT

It is no good selling your goods or services if you do not get paid for them or if your customers take so long to pay that you have to borrow money and pay interest to finance your materials and the wages of your employees.

Accounts receivable is the name given by accountants for the money owed on goods or services which have been invoiced but not yet paid for.

Most small retail shops sell for cash and refuse to give credit. They know that if they begin, some people will never pay them.

You must have clear rules for payment – make sure your customers know them – and stick to them. Then there can be no misunderstanding. (We know that big and important customers like governments will sometimes break your rules, and you cannot refuse them.)

Have your rules clearly printed on quotations and invoices and well displayed in your shop. You can help to speed up payments by offering discounts to those who pay quickly and making the slow payers pay something extra (a penalty). These may be:

HAVE CLEAR RULES FOR PAYMENT AND MAKE SURE YOUR CUSTOMERS KNOW THEM

- discounts – 2½ per cent off for cash or payment within 15 days (see below);

- penalties – 2 per cent interest per calendar month to be charged after 30 days from the date when payment is due.

Try to look ahead. If you must give a big credit, check the customer's record for payments. Your bank can help you. If the person is known as a very bad payer, it may be better to refuse the order. If he or she is someone important who can help you get other orders, you may even have to lose money. You must decide.

DISCOUNTS

Do not forget that your prices must allow for discounts to people who buy big quantities – government contracts, wholesalers and trade customers such as other manufacturers. It is often also trade practice to give a discount (e.g. 2½ per cent) for cash payments which are made within 30 days. This helps to increase the inflow of cash. *Remember:* think out what your discounts can be and what reduction in price you can give to get a big order.

You can also help yourself by sending out your invoices as quickly as possible after the dispatch of the goods – with the goods if you can or by the next post.

▲ DISCOUNTS FOR QUICK PAYMENTS HELP TO GET CASH IN **FAST**

GOOD INVOICING

You can only get your invoices out quickly if you have good records so that information can be quickly and easily put on the invoices.

You should also make sure that your invoices give exact details of what customers are paying for, so that they cannot delay payment by disputing the invoice.

Look at these two invoices:

1

INVOICE

DESCRIPTION	ITEM	TOTAL
Repairs to house, tax included		1,195
	TAX	
	TOTAL	1,195

2

INVOICE

DESCRIPTION	ITEM	TOTAL
Removed cast iron gutters and drain pipe, replaced with PVC.		
Removed 2 panes glass and replaced.		
Removed and replaced skirting in living-room.		
Material : PVC gutters and pipe :	325	325
2 panes glass, 100x600 cm, per piece :	110	220
Wood 18x1.5 cm, 21m per m	10	210
Labour : 10 hours, per hr.	40	400
		1,155
Tax -labour only at 10%	TAX	40
	TOTAL	1,195

If your customer wants to dispute the first invoice, it can waste a lot of time. If the work was done on word of mouth only, you may have to cut the price you ask. In the second invoice, each item is clearly stated. If there are any questions, you can check each item with your customer.

You do not want to take a customer to court. It will surely cost you money. You can buy printed forms with reminders that payments are due. One type has three parts. They can be sent out every 14 days. In each one the wording is tougher. But in the end, you must decide if it is worth taking a non-payer to court.

TO GET YOUR MONEY, BE:

6th April 1986

Dear Mr. Slow,

In checking our ledgers we notice that your account for 40,000 NU has remained unpaid for over two months. We would be grateful to have your cheque in full payment by return of post.

Yours sincerely,

A. Manufacturer

1 STRONG BUT POLITE
▽

20th April 1986

Dear Sir,

In spite of our earlier letter to you, there has been no cheque from you yet, in settlement of your outstanding balance. Please send your cheque immediately upon receipt of this letter, and telephone me to confirm that your cheque is in the post.

Yours faithfully,

A. Manufacturer

2 THEN, TOUGH
▽

4th May 1986

Sir,

In spite of two reminders to you, your outstanding balance still remains unpaid. Unless the amount is settled within seven days of the date on this letter, we will be obliged to initiate legal action for recovery of the debt.

Yours faithfully,

A. Manufacturer

3 THEN, EVEN MORE TOUGH

MANAGEMENT ACCOUNTING

6

Management accounting is using the information from your bookkeeping and other records to see whether your business is doing well or badly.

To be able to decide how your business is doing and whether it is going up or down, you must keep written records. If you do not keep records or if you think the way you keep your business records is poor, study the Bookkeeping section of *Improve your business.*

Good records will help you to make better decisions and manage the business better. You do not have to be an accountant to understand the basics of management accounting.

▲ **WITH GOOD INFORMATION YOU CAN SEE WHERE YOU ARE GOING**

Management accounting provides information which makes it possible for you to know:

● what money has come in and how the money has gone out during a certain period. It tells you also if your business has made a profit or a loss;

● what money and things your business owns and what it owes on a certain date;

● how and when money will come into the business and how and when it will go out during the next few months.

TRY TO FIND OUT:

HOW MONEY CAME IN AND WENT OUT

WHAT YOU OWN AND WHAT YOU OWE

HOW MONEY WILL COME IN AND WILL GO OUT

All the above information you will have if you produce for your business:

● a profit and loss account;

● a balance sheet; and

● a cash budget.

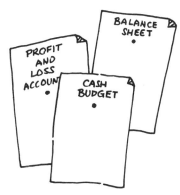

This section of *Improve your business* will help you to put together each of these three documents. You can then use them to manage your business better.

THESE GIVE YOU INFORMATION

THE PROFIT AND LOSS ACCOUNT

The profit and loss account tells you if the business has made a profit or a loss during a certain period (e.g. three months, six months or a year) and if the money which has come into the business during that period is greater or less than the money which has gone out.

Money <u>in</u>   minus   money <u>out</u>   gives   profit

The information about *money in* and *money out* which you write down in your profit and loss account comes from your bookkeeping, mainly from your ledger.

The account in your ledger which tells you what is the amount of *money in* during the period is Sales.

The accounts in your ledger which tell you what are the amounts of *money out* during the period are Raw materials, Wages, Interest, Drawings and Others.

THE LEDGER TELLS YOU ABOUT YOUR MONEY IN AND YOUR MONEY OUT

Let us look at the example of a ledger below:

Money in   **Money out**

Date	Particulars	Id. no.	Cash	Bank	Sales	Raw Mat.	Wages	Loans	Equip-ment	Inter-est	Draw-ings	Others
June												
30					80,000	30,000	12,500			4,000	15,000	6,000

The figure for *money in* (80,000 NU) is obtained by adding up the Sales column.

The figures for *money out* (Raw materials: 30,000 NU; Wages: 12,500 NU; Interest: 4,000 NU; Drawings: 15,000 NU; and Others: 6,000 NU) are obtained by adding up each of these columns in the ledger.

In your business, you also work with four other major things which help you to make your profit. These things are stock, people to whom you owe money (creditors), people who owe you money (debtors) and machines and tools (assets).

If you want to show the true figure for profit in your business, you have to show the increase in value *(money in)* or the decrease in value *(money out)* of these things in your profit and loss account. To record information on each of these things properly, you need to keep four subsidiary books (see the Bookkeeping section of this *Handbook*). These are:

- a stock book;
- an inventory book;
- a purchase journal;
- an invoice book.

▲ GET ADDITIONAL INFORMATION FROM YOUR SUBSIDIARY BOOKS

From the *stock book* you find whether the value of your stock has increased or decreased during the period.

THE STOCK BOOK GIVES CHANGES IN STOCK VALUE

From the *inventory book* you find by how much the value of your machines and other equipment has decreased during the period.

THE INVENTORY BOOK GIVES DECREASES IN VALUE OF EQUIPMENT

From the *purchase journal* you find whether the amount which the business owes to its suppliers has increased or decreased during the period.

THE PURCHASE JOURNAL GIVES CHANGES IN MONEY YOU OWE TO SUPPLIERS

From the *invoice book* you find whether the amount which your customers owe to the business has increased or decreased during the period.

We will now show you how to get the information you need for your profit and loss account out of these four books. Let us take an example of a profit and loss account for the period January to June.

THE INVOICE BOOK GIVES CHANGES IN MONEY OWED TO YOU

FINDING OUT THE CHANGE IN THE VALUE OF STOCK

Whenever you check stock, you write the value of the stock into your stock book.

You need to know the change in the value of stock which has taken place between 1 January and 30 June, as shown below.

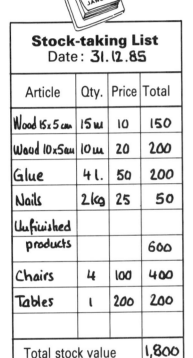

Stock-taking List Date: 31.12.85			
Article	Qty.	Price	Total
Wood 15x5cm	15 m	10	150
Wood 10x5cm	10 m	20	200
Glue	4 l.	50	200
Nails	2 kg	25	50
Unfinished products			600
Chairs	4	100	400
Tables	1	200	200
Total stock value			1,800

Stock-taking List Date: 30.6.86			
Article	Qty.	Price	Total
Wood 15x5cm	10m	10	100
Wood 10x5cm	20m	20	400
Glue	5 l.	60	300
Nails	8 kg	25	200
Unfinished products			400
Chairs	8	100	800
Tables	3	200	600
Total stock value			2,800

OPENING STOCK ON
1 JANUARY: 1,800
▽
STOCK ON
30 JUNE: 2,800
▽
INCREASE IN STOCK
VALUE: 1,000

From the figures given in the stock book, you can see that there has been a 1,000 NU increase in stock. This means that 1,000 NU more has gone into the business. Put it into the *Money in* column of the profit and loss account.

FINDING OUT THE CHANGE IN THE VALUE OF MACHINES AND EQUIPMENT

The machines and equipment you use in the business will sooner or later be worn out. The value of a machine you buy today is, for example, 15,000 NU. After five years of daily use it may be worn out and the value is nil.

It costs you 3,000 NU a year (15,000 NU divided by 5) to

use that particular machine. If you divide 3,000 NU by 2 you will have the cost of the use of that machine for half a year or six months. This is money that goes out of your business. This reduction in value is called "depreciation".

When you buy a new machine you record the purchase value and the year of purchase in your inventory book. At the end of each year you deduct 20 per cent for depreciation. Look at the inventory book below:

Drilling machine	1983
Price	10,000
Depreciation per year	2,000
Value end of 1983	8,000
1984	6,000
1985	4,000
1986	2,000

Turning lathe	1984
Price	25,000
Depreciation per year	5,000
Value end of 1984	20,000
1985	15,000
1986	10,000

Bandsaw	1985
Price	15,000
Depreciation per year	3,000
Value end of 1985	12,000
1986	9,000

Milling machine	1985
Price	25,000
Depreciation per year	5,000
Value end of 1985	20,000
1986	15,000

DEPRECIATION = REDUCTION IN VALUE OF YOUR EQUIPMENT

Total depreciation per year: 15,000 NU; half a year: 7,500 NU

In this example the sum of the depreciations of the four machines is 15,000 NU per year. Divide that amount by 2 and you will have the cost for a six-month period; 7,500 NU.

This is value which has gone out of your machines and equipment. Put it into the *Money out* column of the profit and loss account.

FINDING OUT THE VALUE OF DEBTORS

Whenever you send an invoice to a customer, you keep a copy in the invoice book. Therefore the total amount of money owed by your customers (i.e. the value of your debtors) can be found by adding the amounts on the copies of the unpaid invoices in your invoice book. Do this on 1 January and 30 June, as shown on the next page.

From the invoices you can see that the value of debtors

(i.e. the amounts that customers owe) has increased
from 3,500 NU to 4,500 NU, i.e. by 1,000 NU. This
means that 1,000 NU more has gone into the business.
Put it into the *Money in* column of the profit and loss
account.

FINDING OUT THE VALUE OF CREDITORS

Whenever you receive an invoice from a supplier, you
write the details and the amount into the purchase
journal.

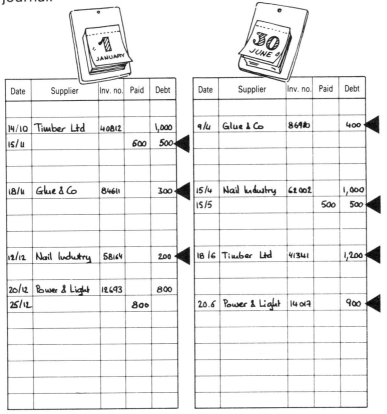

Date	Supplier	Inv. no.	Paid	Debt
14/10	Timber Ltd	40812		1,000
15/11			500	500
18/11	Glue & Co	84611		300
12/12	Nail Industry	58164		200
20/12	Power & Light	12693		800
25/12			800	

Date	Supplier	Inv. no.	Paid	Debt
9/4	Glue & Co	86980		400
15/4	Nail Industry	62002		1,000
15/5			500	500
18/6	Timber Ltd	41341		1,200
20.6	Power & Light	14017		900

**OUTSTANDING
BALANCE AT 1 JAN.:**
500 + 300 + 200
= 1,000

**OUTSTANDING
BALANCE AT
30 JUNE:**
400 + 500 + 1,200
+ 900 = 3,000

94

The total amount of money that you owe to your suppliers (i.e. the value of your creditors) can be found at any time by adding up the unpaid amounts in the purchase journal.

Do this on 1 January and 30 June, as shown on the previous page.

According to the figures in the purchase journal, the value of creditors (i.e. the amount you owe to your suppliers) has increased from 1,000 NU to 3,000 NU, i.e. by 2,000 NU. This means that 2,000 NU has gone out of the business. Put it into the *Money out* column of the profit and loss account.

HOW TO CONSTRUCT YOUR PROFIT AND LOSS ACCOUNT

Now we have all the figures necessary to draw up the following profit and loss account:

	Profit and loss account		
	1 January-30 June 1986		
	Money in		
	Sales	80,000	
	Change in stocks	1,000	
	Change in debtors	1,000	
			82,000
Less:	*Money out*		
	Raw materials	30,000	
	Wages	12,500	
	Interest	4,000	
	Drawings	15,000	
	Others	6,000	
	Change in creditors	2,000	
	Depreciation	7,500	
			77,000
Gives:	*Profit*		5,000

▲ NOW I KNOW IF MY BUSINESS HAS MADE A PROFIT!

Do this every six months and see your progress.

THE BALANCE SHEET

A balance sheet shows the financial position of a business at one particular moment in time. It shows what a business owns and what it owes at that moment or, in other words, its *assets* and *liabilities*.

What the business owns (assets)

Cash

Bank

Debtors (people who owe money to the business)

Stocks

Equipment

What the business owes (liabilities)

Creditors (people to whom the business owes money)

Loans (owed to the bank)

Owners' capital (owed to the owner)

Retained profits (owed to the owner)

Like the profit and loss account, the balance sheet is drawn up with the aid of the accounts from your bookkeeping system.

The accounts in your ledger that tell you about your *assets* are Cash, Bank and Equipment.

The account in your ledger that tells you about your *liabilities* is the Loan account.

Let us look at the example of a ledger below:

THE **LEDGER** TELLS YOU ABOUT YOUR **ASSETS** AND **LIABILITIES**

▼ **ASSETS**   ▽**LIABILITIES**

Date	Particulars	Id. no.	Cash	Bank	Sales	Raw Mat.	Wages	Loans	Equip-ment	Inter-est	Draw-ings	Others
June												
30			4,000	5,000				40,000	51,000			

The figures for *assets* are Cash (4,000 NU), Bank (5,000 NU) and Equipment (51,000 NU).

The figure for *liabilities* is Loans (40,000 NU).

But there are a few more things to consider before you can draw up your balance sheet:

- the depreciation of machinery and equipment;

- the value of the stock;

- how much your customers owe to the business – your debtors;

- how much the business owes its suppliers – your creditors;

- how much money you, the owner, have put into the business – the owner's capital.

We will now show you how to get this additional information.

▲ GET ADDITIONAL INFORMATION FROM YOUR SUBSIDIARY BOOKS

FINDING OUT THE DEPRECIATION OF MACHINERY AND EQUIPMENT

When we drew up a profit and loss account we had to consider the reduction in the value of your machines and equipment. This was called depreciation. When you are about to draw up a balance sheet you must also put in this reduction in value. Look at the sheets from the inventory book shown below:

Drilling machine	1983
Price	10,000
Depreciation	
per year	2,000
Value end of 1983	8,000
1984	6,000
1985	4,000
1986	2,000

Turning lathe	1984
Price	25,000
Depreciation	
per year	5,000
Value end of 1984	20,000
1985	15,000
1986	10,000

Bandsaw	1985
Price	15,000
Depreciation	
per year	3,000
Value end of 1985	12,000
1986	9,000

Milling machine	1985
Price	25,000
Depreciation	
per year	5,000
Value end of 1985	20,000
1986	15,000

Total value at end of 1985: 51,000

THE **INVENTORY BOOK** GIVES YOU THE VALUE OF YOUR EQUIPMENT

The total value of the four machines at the end of 1985 is 51,000 NU. The total depreciation per year is 15,000 NU. If we want to draw up a balance sheet on 30 June 1986 (six months after the end of 1985), we have to reduce the value noted in the ledger by 7,500 NU (half of 15,000 NU).

Whenever you draw up a balance sheet, you enter the amount of depreciation (for the period since the last balance sheet) in the ledger. Put it into the *out* column of the Equipment account and into the *in* column of the Others account, noting that it is depreciation. You make the entry like this:

MAKE THE ENTRY FOR DEPRECIATION IN THE LEDGER

DATE	PARTICULARS	ID.NO.
	Depreciation ½	

OUT ▼   IN ▼

EQUIPMENT				OTHERS	
In	Out			In	Out
51,000					
	7,500			7,500	
43,500					

The depreciation reduces the value of the equipment in your assets to:

51,000 NU − 7,500 NU = 43,500 NU.

THE VALUE OF YOUR EQUIPMENT DECLINES MONTH BY MONTH

FINDING OUT THE VALUE OF STOCK

Look at the following stock-taking list which was also used to draw up the profit and loss account:

The total value of the stock at 30 June is 2,800 NU. This figure is an *asset.*

Stock-taking List Date:			
Article	Qty.	Price	Total
Total stock value			

Stock-taking List Date: 30.6.86			
Article	Qty.	Price	Total
Wood 15×5 cm	10m	10	100
Wood 10×5 cm	20m	20	400
Glue	5ℓ	60	300
Nails	8kg	25	200
Unfinished products			400
Chairs	8	100	800
Tables	3	200	600
Total stock value			2,800

THE **STOCK BOOK** GIVES YOU THE VALUE OF YOUR STOCK

FINDING OUT THE VALUE OF DEBTORS

You can find out the value of your debtors on 30 June from the invoice book, as shown above under "Profit and loss account". Add up all the unpaid amounts on the invoices outstanding to arrive at the total amount.

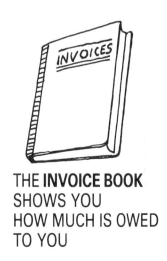

THE **INVOICE BOOK** SHOWS YOU HOW MUCH IS OWED TO YOU

The total value of unpaid amounts at 30 June is 4,500 NU. This figure is an *asset.*

FINDING OUT THE VALUE OF CREDITORS

You can find out the value of your creditors from the purchase journal, as shown above under "Profit and loss account". Add up all unpaid and partly paid invoices to arrive at the total amount.

Date	Supplier	Inv. no.	Paid	Debt
9/4	Glue & Co	86920		400
15/4	Nail Industry	62002		1,000
15/5			500	500
18/6	Timber Ltd	41341		1,200
20/6	Power & Light	14017		900

Outstanding balance at 30 June:

400 + 500 + 1,200 + 900 = 3,000.

The total value of unpaid amounts at 30 June is therefore 3,000 NU. This figure is a *liability*.

THE **PURCHASE JOURNAL** SHOWS YOU HOW MUCH IS OWED TO YOUR SUPPLIERS

FINDING OUT THE AMOUNT OF THE OWNER'S CAPITAL

You probably have a rough idea about how much money you have put into the business yourself. However, if you are not satisfied with a rough estimate you should keep a record in a book, e.g. a business notebook. In this you can record every change in the amount of money that you have put into the business as shown on the next page.

Money put in by myself when started 1978	6,000 NU
Extra money put in 1986	5,800 NU

The total amount of money that you have put into the business up to 30 June is 11,800 NU. The business owes you this amount. It is a *liability* of the business.

THE **BUSINESS NOTEBOOK** GIVES YOU THE FIGURE FOR OWNER'S CAPITAL

HOW TO CONSTRUCT YOUR BALANCE SHEET

Now we have all the figures necessary to draw up the following balance sheet:

Balance sheet 30 June 1986

Assets		Liabilities	
Cash	4,000	Creditors	3,000
Bank	5,000	Loans	40,000
Debtors	4,500	Owner's capital	11,800
Stock	2,800	Profit made	
Equipment 51,000		1 Jan.-30 June	5,000
Less: 7,500			
	43,500		
	59,800		59,800

The figure for profit, 5,000 NU, is obtained from the profit and loss account. Add the amount of profit to the liabilities side. It is again money which the business owes to you.

As you can see, the two sides of the balance sheet end up with the same amount. They are in balance.

▲ NOW I KNOW MY POSITION!

THE CASH FLOW BUDGET

A cash flow budget is a plan which shows how you think cash will flow into the business (cash receipts) and out of the business (cash payments) month by month during a future period.

If a business is to keep out of trouble, it must have enough cash flowing in to pay the day-to-day expenses like wages, suppliers, rent and electricity. Many businesses have gone bankrupt because they did not have enough cash even when they had full order books. If customers do not pay on time and creditors will not wait, and if the bank will not help, a business is in trouble.

A cash flow budget helps you to forecast or estimate your future cash situation. The information for your cash flow budget comes from your bookkeeping, mainly the ledger. By studying what has happened in the past you can forecast what may happen in the future. The longer you keep good records the better your forecasts will be.

It is often enough to write out the cash flow budget for the next six-month period. But do not wait until the end of the six-month period until you write out your next forecast. Sit down after three months and try to estimate ahead for another six-month period.

Look at the table on the next page. This is an example of a cash flow budget. We show you how it is filled in, step by step. Follow the directions given on the next few pages.

▲ A CASH FLOW
BUDGET IS
A FORECAST OF
YOUR FUTURE
CASH SITUATION

**WILL YOU HAVE
ENOUGH CASH
EACH MONTH
DURING THE NEXT
SIX-MONTH PERIOD?**

THE CASH FLOW BUDGET

		January	February	March	April	May	June
RECEIPTS	**1** Money present at start of month						
	2 Cash sales						
	3 Cash from credit sales						
	4 Other money in						
	Money in this month						
PAYMENTS	**5** Cash purchases						
	6 Cash paid for credit purchases						
	7 Wages						
	8 Drawings						
	9 Loan repayment						
	10 Interest						
	11 Others						
	12 Planned investments						
	Money out this month						
	Money present at end of month						

HOW TO CONSTRUCT YOUR CASH FLOW BUDGET

1. Money present at start of month

How much money do you have in the cash box and in your bank account at the beginning of January? Add the amounts together and enter the total, 7,000 NU, into the first row as follows:

CASH: 2,000 NU +
CURRENT ACCOUNT:
5,000 NU

	January	February	March	April	May	June
Money present at start of month	7,000 ◄					

Now, look at the receipts.

2. Cash sales

Check your past cash sales from the cash receipt copies in the voucher file and then try to estimate the figure of cash sales that you will make in each month.

	January	February	March	April	May	June
Cash sales	7,500 ▲	6,000 ▲	6,000 ▲	6,000 ▲	7,500 ▲	12,500 ▲

3. Credit sales

Again check in your invoice book to see how much you have sold on credit during each month of the past year. Estimate the amount you think you will actually sell on credit (i.e. the amount for which you will issue invoices) during each of the next six months. Enter these estimates into the small triangle in the top left-hand corner of each box.

	January	February	March	April	May	June
Cash from credit sales	2,500	2,000	2,500	2,500	1,500	2,000 ◄

You use these figures when you calculate the cash received from credit sales for each month. For example, if customers pay you a month after they receive your invoice you can then fill in the "cash from credit sales" row as follows:

	January	February	March	April	May	June
Cash from credit sales	2,500	2,000 ◄ 2,500	2,500 ◄ 2,000	2,500 ◄ 2,500	1,500 ◄ 2,500	2,000 ◄ 1,500

Remember that if you made credit sales during the previous months, you will also need to include the cash received in January from these sales.

4. Other money in

If you are expecting to get cash as a result of the sale of a machine or other assets, enter your estimate of that amount in the column of the month when you expect the cash: e.g. you sell a machine for cash in April for 12,000 NU.

	January	February	March	April	May	June
Other money in				12,000 ◀		

Now, look at the payments.

5. Cash purchases

Try to estimate how much you will spend on raw materials and parts for each of the next six months: e.g. January: 2,500 NU; February: 3,750 NU; March: 5,000 NU; April: 3,750 NU; May: 3,750 NU; and June: 6,250 NU. Now try to work out how much of these purchases you will pay in cash. Enter these figures into the row for cash purchases as in the example below:

CASH PURCHASES

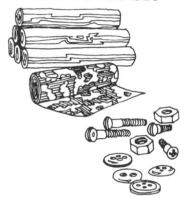

	January	February	March	April	May	June
Cash purchases	2,000 ▲	3,000 ▲	4,000 ▲	3,000 ▲	3,000 ▲	5,000 ▲

6. Cash paid for credit purchases

Deduct the figures which you entered into row no. 5 above from your estimates of your *total* purchases for each month, and enter the results in the small triangle in the top left-hand corner of each box in row no. 6. For example, the figure for January is 2,500 NU, minus 2,000 NU (cash purchases), which equals 500 NU.

CREDIT PURCHASES

	January	February	March	April	May	June	
Cash paid for credit purchases	500	750	1,000	750	750	1,250	◀

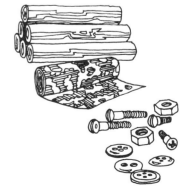

You use these figures when you calculate how much of your credit purchases you will pay in cash each month. For example, if each time you are going to pay two months after you have received the invoice, row no. 6 will look as shown on the next page.

	January	February	March	April	May	June
Cash paid for credit purchases	500	750	1,000	750	750	1,250
			500	750	1,000	750

7. Wages

Look at your payroll and work out how many people you will employ and how much their wages will be for each month.

Enter the total wage bill for each month like this:

	January	February	March	April	May	June
Wages	2,000	2,000	2,000	2,000	2,000	2,000

8. Drawings

Estimate how much you will draw from your business each month as a salary for yourself. Enter your estimates like this:

	January	February	March	April	May	June
Drawings	3,000	3,000	3,000	3,000	3,000	3,000

9 and 10. Loan repayment and interest

Check your loan document. Find out when payments are due and how much they are. For example, you make your loan repayment quarterly, in March and June. Each repayment is 1,000 NU.

	January	February	March	April	May	June
Loan repayment			1,000			1,000

You make the interest payments on a monthly basis. In this case, enter the amount you pay each month, e.g. 600 NU for January, February and March and 550 NU for April, May and June.

	January	February	March	April	May	June
Interest	600	600	600	550	550	550

11. Others

Enter your estimate of how much you will spend in each month for all the other expenses which normally arise when you run a business, e.g. rent, telephone, insurance, electricity.

	January	February	March	April	May	June
Others	1,500	1,500	3,000	1,500	1,500	3,000

12. Planned investments

If you have planned any new investment, estimate when and how much you are going to pay:

	January	February	March	April	May	June
Planned investments				5,000 ◀		

We have now entered all the figures necessary to complete our cash flow budget. The cash flow budget now looks as shown on page 108.

All that is now left for us to do are some additions and subtractions:

- Start with the column for January. Add rows 1, 2, 3 and 4 together. Enter the total, 14,500 NU, in the row called "Money in this month".

- Next, add up all the payments for January (rows 5-12). Enter the total, 9,100 NU, in the row called "Money out this month".

- Subtract as follows:

	Money in this month	14,500
−	Money out this month	9,100
=	Money present at end of month	5,400

Enter this figure in the bottom row. Also enter it in row 1, in the column for February.

- Add up the figures for February to June in the same way as you did for January. The result is your six-month cash flow budget as shown on page 109.

THE CASH FLOW BUDGET

		January	February	March	April	May	June
RECEIPTS	1	Money present at start of month	7,000					
	2	Cash sales	7,500	6,000	6,000	6,000	7,500	12,500
	3	Cash from credit sales	2,500 / –	2,000 / 2,500	2,500 / 2,000	2,500 / 2,500	1,500 / 2,500	2,000 / 1,500
	4	Other money in				12.000		
		Money in this month						
PAYMENTS	5	Cash purchases	2,000	3,000	4,000	3,000	3,000	5,000
	6	Cash paid for credit purchases	500 / –	750 / –	1,000 / 500	750 / 750	750 / 1,000	1,250 / 750
	7	Wages	2,000	2,000	2,000	2,000	2,000	2,600
	8	Drawings	3,000	3,000	3,000	3,000	3,000	3,000
	9	Loan repayment			1,000			1,000
	10	Interest	600	600	600	550	550	550
	11	Others	1,500	1,500	3,000	1,500	1,500	3,000
	12	Planned investments				5,000		
		Money out this month						
		Money present at end of month						

THE CASH FLOW BUDGET

		January	February	March	April	May	June
RECEIPTS	1	Money present at start of month	7,000	5,400	3,800	-2,300	2,400	1,350
	2	Cash sales	7,500	6,000	6,000	6,000	7,500	12,500
	3	Cash from credit sales	-	2,500	2,000	2,500	2,500	1,500
	4	Other money in				12,000		
		Money in this month	14,500	13,900	11,800	18,200	12,400	15,350
PAYMENTS	5	Cash purchases	2,000	3,000	4,000	3,000	3,000	5,000
	6	Cash paid for credit purchases	-	-	500	750	1,000	750
	7	Wages	2,000	2,600	2,000	2,000	2,000	2,000
	8	Drawings	3,000	3,000	3,000	3,000	3,000	3,000
	9	Loan repayment			1,000			1,000
	10	Interest	600	600	600	550	550	550
	11	Others	1,500	1,500	3,000	1,500	1,500	3,000
	12	Planned investments				5,000		
		Money out this month	9,100	10,100	14,100	15,800	11,050	15,300
		Money present at end of month	5,400	3,800	-2,300	2,400	1,350	50

The cash flow budget shown on page 109 is a good example of what happens when a business does not have enough cash. You can see that, at the beginning of April, the business is actually 2,300 NU in deficit, and that by the end of June it has only 50 NU in hand. By making up a cash flow budget beforehand, you are able to see in advance the cash problems that you may run into. Take action in good time to avoid such a dangerous situation.

▲ **YOUR CASH FLOW BUDGET HELPS YOU TO SEE YOUR CASH SITUATION AND TAKE ACTION**

OFFICE WORK

7

The information centre of your business is the office. It is the first contact made between customers and your business, as well as the store for your bookkeeping and written work about your business.

CONTACT WITH CUSTOMERS

The person who runs your office will usually be the one who answers telephone calls. Train her or him to do so clearly and efficiently. The voice on the telephone may be the first impression that people gain of your business. Remember, the staff who answer the telephone can create or destroy the image of efficiency which you are working hard to establish. Careless handling of a telephone call can make customers impatient and even result in the loss of business.

▲ **REMEMBER**: THE FIRST IMPRESSION OF YOUR BUSINESS MAY BE HOW THE TELEPHONE IS ANSWERED

The following points are a guide to good telephone technique:

● Arrange that the telephone is answered promptly and politely. "Good morning, Betterwork Products" is much more efficient than just "Betterwork Products", and simply saying "Hello" is of no help at all.

● Some telephone operators answer by saying: "Hold the line please". This is impolite and may lose business for you. Instruct your office staff so that they avoid such conduct. It is not professional.

● Members of staff who also have telephone extensions must be taught to answer the phone in the same way.

● Staff who are slow to answer the telephone, or who do not meet their promises to make return telephone calls to customers as quickly as they can, could also lose business for you.

THIS CONDUCT CAN LOSE YOU BUSINESS

BUSINESS LETTERS

People who run their own businesses need to communicate with customers or suppliers by means of letters. The business letter may often be the first impression that people will gain of your business.

To produce good business letters, you must remember the following points:

- The first impression of a letter is important. Check the layout and presentation of your letters. Do they look good? Is the writing or typing neat? Is the letter-head neat and clean?

- Think out the objective of each letter you write. Is it a letter asking for money, a letter ordering goods, a complaint about poor service or a letter asking for a loan? State your objective clearly and briefly.

- Begin your letter with the main idea that you want to put over and avoid just writing pleasant words.

- Before you dictate a letter, write down all the relevant information. The easiest way to do this is to list the points you wish to make and build your paragraphs around these points.

REMEMBER:
THE FIRST IMPRESSION OF YOUR BUSINESS MAY BE HOW YOUR LETTERS LOOK

YOUR INFORMATION STORE

The office is the place where you store all the written information and records of your business. It is very important to keep these things together neatly so that your office staff can find the information easily.

This means that there must be a system for collecting and storing the various types of paperwork such as letters, invoices, receipts, orders and so on. There must be one place and one place only for each of the different types of paperwork. Tidiness is essential to run your business efficiently.

Remember: The tidiness of your office may also be the first direct impression gained by a customer who visits you personally.

YOUR OFFICE IS YOUR INFORMATION STORE: **KEEP IT TIDY**

FILING

To collect and store the paperwork of your business, you need to file the different types of papers. Do not spend a lot of money on this.

Box files are good but expensive. Simple folders are cheap. Holes can be punched in the folders and in the documents. The documents can then be fastened into the folders with a string. A simple filing system of this type may be adequate for your business.

It is essential to keep the filing up to date. Time should be set aside each day for filing the documents, and it must never be missed. Documents should be sorted in separate files under the different file headings. You can have separate files for the following items.

DO YOUR FILING
THIS WAY

OR **THIS WAY**

BUT DO IT
EVERY DAY

WAGES

Information for calculating pay should include wage lists with the names of the workers together with their details, their total pay, deductions from pay and net pay received.

EXPENSES CLAIMS

Where there is a lot of travel by employees and the business pays for that travel, copies of the claims for expenses must be kept.

DATA FOR INVOICING

Information on each completed job must be stored (e.g. the details of labour and material or the customer's order).

COPIES OF YOUR OWN INVOICES

When your typist types invoices, two copies should be filed alphabetically in a file called "Invoices outstanding.'' This is an essential file because it represents money which will come into your business when the customer pays. When the payment is received from the customer, the two copies are stamped ''Paid''. One copy is moved from the *Invoices outstanding file* to the *Invoices paid file,* which is also kept in alphabetical order. It is essential that the other copy of the same invoice is filed in number order, usually in a *Voucher file.*

VOUCHERS

Some businesses use one General voucher file, in which all paid vouchers are stored. When money is paid or received, the relevant voucher is marked ''Paid'', a number is written on it and it is filed in the Voucher file in number order.

SUPPLIERS' INVOICES

These are invoices which you have received from suppliers of goods or raw materials (e.g. material for making your product) or from businesses which have supplied you with services (e.g. motor car repairs, electricity or stationery). These invoices are filed alphabetically. Many small businesses maintain two files:

● Unpaid invoices from suppliers; and
● Suppliers' invoices paid.

Once the payment is made, a note is written on the unpaid invoice stating when and by whom payment was authorised and that the details have been checked. That invoice is then transferred to the file labelled ''Suppliers' invoices paid,'' again in alphabetical order by supplier's name.

TAX FILE

This file is for all tax matters relating to your business and employees.

▲ **HOW TO DO YOUR INVOICING:**

TYPE THREE COPIES OF THE INVOICE
▽

GIVE ONE COPY TO YOUR CUSTOMER AND FILE THE OTHERS
▽

WHEN THE CUSTOMER PAYS, STAMP THEM ''PAID'' AND FILE THEM AGAIN

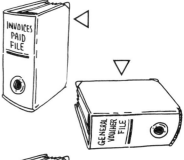

△ KEEP SUPPLIERS' INVOICES IN SEPARATE FILES

LETTER FILES

Even in the smallest office there should be files for incoming letters and copies of replies. Letters can be filed alphabetically according to the first letter (A, B, C, etc.) of the client's name.

LETTER FILES

THESE ARE THE FILES YOU NEED

THE BUSINESS FILE

There are many more files you can buy, depending on the size and kind of your business. We will not describe these in full, but there is one particular file which we mention because it is so important for your success in business. This file is called "The business" and should be used to file the originals of all important documents relating to the business such as annual reports, board meetings, insurance policies and important contracts. The file with the originals of the documents should be kept in a safe and the file with the copies can be kept with the other files.

KEEP YOUR BUSINESS DOCUMENTS SAFE

OFFICE MACHINES

There are many machines available which can help with the office work (e.g. calculators and typewriters). Many of these machines are very expensive. However, an essential purchase for your business as soon as possible should be a typewriter. Buy the best you can afford because the letters from your office create an impression of your business in the minds of customers. As you expand, you may think it is necessary to invest in a photocopying machine. However, make sure you have enough work to make such a purchase useful; otherwise, continue to take your work to a photocopying shop until the amount of photocopying work increases.

FIRST, BUY A **TYPEWRITER: BUY THE BEST YOU CAN AFFORD**

A **PHOTOCOPYING MACHINE** IS USEFUL IF YOU HAVE ENOUGH WORK

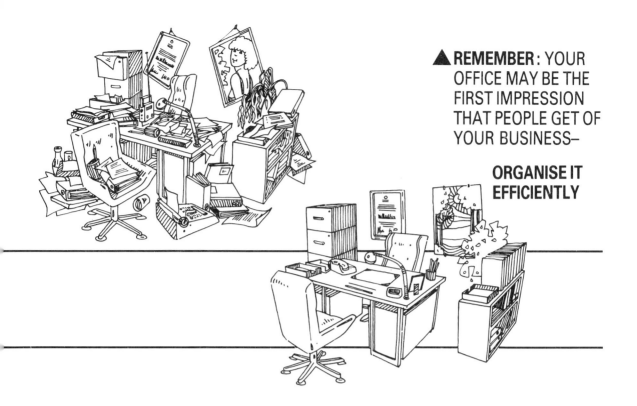

▲ **REMEMBER**: YOUR
OFFICE MAY BE THE
FIRST IMPRESSION
THAT PEOPLE GET OF
YOUR BUSINESS–

**ORGANISE IT
EFFICIENTLY**

PLANNING

8

Nothing in the world stands still for ever. Some businesses may go along for years in the same way and make a good living for their owners, but sooner or later they will find that they must change.

This is because:

- customers no longer want your goods – they want something new or something better;

- other businesses have come up which promote their products more actively than you do;

- machines and equipment have grown old, cost more to run and break down frequently. They must be replaced;

- the business is growing and it is necessary to decide how it shall grow and how much.

If you are wise, you will begin to think about the future long before you must do something, so that you have time to prepare yourself. Most of your days are busy with running your business, but there are evenings and other times when you can stop and ask yourself: "Where do I go from here?"

You must start to make plans for your sales and costs for the months ahead, and think of new investments you will have to make in order to carry out your plans.

The sooner you start to think about the future, the more time you have to look around, get advice and find the best way to go.

▲ BE WISE: **THINK ABOUT THE FUTURE**

ASK YOURSELF: "WHERE DO I GO FROM HERE?"

PLANNING SALES AND COSTS

Planning is thinking out, and then working out in detail, what you intend to do in a future

period of time and how you expect to get there.

Planning for your business is similar to what you do when you set out on a journey. Before you start on a journey you plan or think out three things:

1. *Where you want to go:*
   Before you start out on any journey you think out where you want to go, e.g. from London to Nairobi.

2. *How you will get there:*
   Then you think out in detail how you will get there, e.g. by plane, boat or over land.
   You also choose which route you will follow, e.g. London-Paris-Rome-Nairobi or London-Nairobi direct.

3. *How long the journey will take, and the distance:*
   You think out how long it will take, for example:

	Time taken	*Distance*
London – Paris	½ hour	500 km
Paris – Rome	1½ hours	1,500 km
Rome – Nairobi	6 hours	6,000 km
Total	8 hours	8,000 km

Planning the future of your business is the same:

1. You think out or forecast where you want your business to go, e.g. you think you will get sales of 100,000 NU next year.

2. Then you think out how you will get there, e.g. you will sell more of the products you already make – chairs – and add a new product – beds.

3. Lastly, you think out how long it will take and what you should achieve, e.g. you will make sales of 8,000 NU per month during ten months, but in each of November and December you intend to sell 10,000 NU. The annual total will therefore be 100,000 NU.

PLANNING A BUSINESS IS LIKE PLANNING A JOURNEY

ASK YOURSELF:

- WHERE DO I WANT TO GO?
- HOW WILL I GET THERE?
- HOW LONG WILL IT TAKE ME?

BUSINESS PLAN

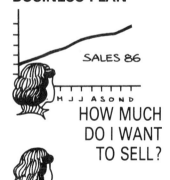

SALES 86

HOW MUCH DO I WANT TO SELL?

HOW WILL I DO IT?

HOW LONG WILL IT TAKE?

YOUR BUSINESS PLAN

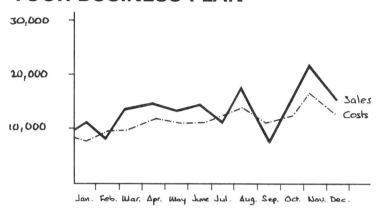

You should make a plan for your business for the next year (e.g. 1987) or, if your business is growing fast, for the next three years. You write your plan down on paper. What you write must be your best estimate of what you think you can achieve with the resources you have in your business, e.g. with the machines, workers and cash that you have *plus your own ability.*

Your business plan is your estimate of the sales, costs and profit which you think you can achieve.

You estimate what is likely to happen to three basic parts of your business:

- the sales;
- the direct costs; and
- the indirect costs.

If you estimate these three elements reasonably accurately, you will have a good idea of how much profit you are likely to make.

YOUR **BUSINESS PLAN** IS YOUR ESTIMATE OF FUTURE **SALES, COSTS** AND **PROFIT**

ESTIMATING THE SALES

Sit down and work out what you believe the sales are likely to be during the next year, i.e. for the 12-month period 1 January-31 December. You do this using your knowledge of the past year. When you do this, you are making what is called a *sales forecast.*

The most important thing about any sales forecast is that, if all goes well, it must be possible to achieve the figure which you estimate or guess. If it is just not possible, then that is not forecasting – it is dreaming. For example, if the business which you are in is producing stools and you have sold 2,500 of them at 40 NU (total sales 100,000 NU) in 1986, then it may be possible for your business to sell 3,000 in 1987 with extra sales push and some luck, but it would not be wise to make plans to sell 10,000 stools in 1987. That is unrealistic. Your business does not have the workers, the machines or even the money to expand as fast as that.

It will be necessary to forecast the expected number of stools which you will sell in the next year, and also their value. Let us assume that you agree on a sales forecast figure of 3,000 for 1987. During 1986 you improved the quality of your stools by using better-quality wood, and made them more attractive by using brighter paint. As a result you sold more of them during the last few months of the year. Therefore you estimate that you can charge a price of 50 NU per stool for 1987.

Your sales forecast for 1987 is now:

Estimated no. of stools		Selling price		Expected sales for next year
3,000	×	50 NU	=	150,000 NU

Once you have this figure, you must then decide what your sales will be during each month of the year. You know that sales are roughly the same in each month, apart from November when your sales are three times greater than normal, and April, when they are usually a little higher than normal. The first stage in making up your business plan is to fill in the monthly sales figures, as shown below.

TO MAKE A SALES FORECAST:

1 ESTIMATE HOW MANY PRODUCTS YOU WILL MAKE AND SELL

2 ESTIMATE THE PRICE

3 MULTIPLY THE NUMBER OF PRODUCTS BY THE PRICE

ALLOCATE YOUR ESTIMATE OF TOTAL SALES OVER THE DIFFERENT MONTHS
▽

ENTER THESE FIGURES INTO YOUR **BUSINESS PLAN**
▽

Details	Jan.	Feb.	Mar.	Apr.	May	June	July	Aug.	Sep.	Oct.	Nov.	Dec.	Total
Sales	10,000	10,000	10,000	20,000	10,000	10,000	10,000	10,000	10,000	10,000	30,000	10,000	150,000

ESTIMATING THE DIRECT COSTS

The next stage is to estimate the costs of production, or *direct costs*. These are the costs of labour and materials used in actually making the stools. First, let us look at your production plan. You plan to make 3,000 stools over 12 months. You could produce each month the number you plan to sell in that month.

However, this would mean paying excessive overtime in April and November, which would be expensive.

ESTIMATE YOUR **DIRECT COSTS:** COST OF LABOUR AND COST OF RAW MATERIALS

You could get the lowest production costs by making the same number of stools each month. This number would be:

$$\frac{3,000}{12} = 250.$$

On the other hand, this involves a certain amount of "manufacturing for stock" (i.e. making stools that will remain in stock for several months before being sold). This could lead to "cash flow" problems, with cash flowing out to pay for labour and materials long before cash flows in from sales. This in turn could mean the need for a loan or an overdraft, and thus extra interest payments. So although making 250 stools each month may mean the lowest production cost, it does not mean the lowest total costs. In addition, the production workers each have to have three weeks' holiday during the year, so the idea of making the same number of stools each month is not very practical.

You know that with five production workers you can produce 220 units per month without needing overtime work (overtime is paid at 50 per cent more than regular time). You are going to take on a sixth production worker. You estimate that during the first few months of the year you are able to produce 250 units per month without paying overtime and after that, when the new worker is fully trained, 270 units. In November, to meet increased demand in December, you decide to produce 360 stools by paying overtime. Since December contains a third week's holiday, and the peak demand will be over, you aim to produce only 230 stools.

You now produce the following production plan:

▲ ONCE YOU KNOW YOUR **SALES** AND **DIRECT COSTS** YOU CAN ESTIMATE YOUR **GROSS PROFIT**

REMEMBER: SALES LESS DIRECT COSTS GIVES GROSS PROFIT

Month	Starting stock	Production	Sold	Ending stock	Comments
Jan.	30	250	200	80	30 units in stock
Feb.	80	250	200	130	at start of year
March	130	250	200	180	
April	180	250	400	30	
May	30	200	200	30	One production
June	30	200	200	30	worker on leave
July	30	200	200	30	during this period
Aug.	30	270	200	100	
Sept.	100	270	200	170	
Oct.	170	270	200	240	
Nov.	240	360	600	0	
Dec.	0	230	200	30	

Now consider the production costs. The hourly wage rate, including holiday pay and all other fringe benefits, was 4.50 NU and your records of the last few months showed that each stool took 3.6 work-hours to produce. You expect that this will rise by 6-7 per cent during the next three months while the new worker gets used to the job, but this would be offset by some new tools which you will introduce to speed up the manufacturing operations. You estimate that for January, February and March you should allow 3.7 work-hours per stool, and after that 3.5 work-hours. From July you decide to give the workers a wage rise, bringing the hourly wage rate to 4.80 NU.

Now you can calculate your labour costs per stool:

- January, February and March:
  4.50 NU × 3.7 = 16.65 NU;

- April, May and June:
  4.50 NU × 3.5 = 15.75 NU;

- July to December:
  4.80 NU × 3.5 = 16.80 NU.

Multiply these costs by the number of stools you plan to produce each month to find your monthly labour costs.

You have also calculated that materials (wood, paint, glue, etc.) amounted to a cost of 9.70 NU per stool. You have a guarantee from your suppliers that they will not raise prices this year. Multiply the cost of materials by the number of stools you plan to produce for each month.

You can now fill in the next few lines of your business plan.

	Details	Jan.	Feb.	Mar.	Apr.	May	June	July	Aug.	Sep.	Oct.	Nov.	Dec.	Total
	Sales	10,000	10,000	10,000	20,000	10,000	10,000	10,000	10,000	10,000	10,000	30,000	10,000	150,000
Less:	Production costs of which:													
	Labour	4,163	4,163	4,163	3,938	3,150	3,150	3,360	4,536	4,536	4,536	6,048	3,864	49,607
	Materials	2,425	2,425	2,425	2,425	1,940	1,940	1,940	2,619	2,619	2,619	3,492	2,231	29,100
Gives: Gross profit		3,412	3,412	3,412	13,637	4,910	4,910	4,700	2,845	2,845	2,845	20,460	3,905	71,293

ESTIMATING THE INDIRECT COSTS

Now you have to prepare estimates of your *indirect costs*. The biggest indirect costs are for the supervisor, who receives 950 NU per month, and your secretary (part-time) who receives 350 NU per month. So indirect wages are 1,300 NU per month.

SUPERVISOR: 950 NU

Then there are all the other overhead costs. Looking at your accounts for the previous year you find the following:

- Insurance   500
- Postage   800
- Telephone   150
- Electricity   800
- Water   180
- Stationery   420
- Travel   840
- Sundries   820

Consider these one by one. There will be some increase because of inflation (which is, say, 10 per cent per year) and because you are now doing more business.

SECRETARY: 350 NU

Insurance

After a talk with the insurance agent you learn that insurance costs will increase to 750 NU. This is to be paid in two instalments of 375 NU in March and September.

Postage

No increase in postal rates is expected. You allow 900 NU for postage, or 75 NU each month.

Telephone

Telephone rates are expected to increase by 20 per cent. You allow 150 NU plus 20 per cent (i.e. 180 NU) for telephone costs, or 30 NU every two months.

Electricity

Electricity rates are to go up by 10 per cent, and you think you should allow another 10 per cent for increased use. This will come to 800 NU plus 20 per cent, making 960 NU, or 240 NU every three months.

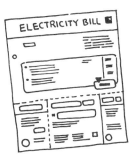

Water

You have no information about a water rate increase, but you reckon that you should allow for an increase of about 10 per cent, say to 200 NU, or 50 NU every three months.

Stationery

You allow an increase of about 20 per cent, to 504 NU, stationery costs. This comes to 42 NU per month.

Travel

These costs can be held to about the same level as last year: 840 NU, or 70 NU per month.

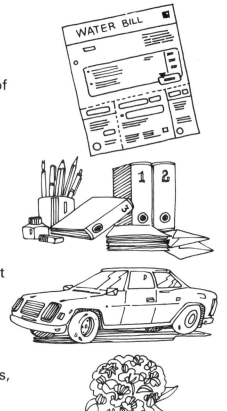

Sundries

These will rise at about the same rate as inflation (10 per cent). You decide to allow 900 NU for sundries, or 75 NU per month.

You are now ready to complete your business plan as follows:

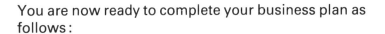

	Details	Jan.	Feb.	Mar.	Apr.	May	June	July	Aug.	Sep.	Oct.	Nov.	Dec.	Total
	Sales	10,000	10,000	10,000	20,000	10,000	10,000	10,000	10,000	10,000	10,000	30,000	10,000	150,000
Less:	Production costs of which:													
	Labour	4,163	4,163	4,163	3,938	3,150	3,150	3,360	4,536	4,536	4,536	6,048	3,864	49,607
	Materials	2,425	2,425	2,425	2,425	1,940	1,940	1,940	2,619	2,619	2,619	3,492	2,231	29,100
Gives:	Gross profit	3,412	3,412	3,412	13,637	4,910	4,910	4,700	2,845	2,845	2,845	20,460	3,905	71,293
Less:	Indirect costs of which:													
	Staff wages	1,300	1,300	1,300	1,300	1,300	1,300	1,300	1,300	1,300	1,300	1,300	1,300	15,600
	Insurance			375						375				750
	Postage	75	75	75	75	75	75	75	75	75	75	75	75	900
	Telephone		30		30		30		30		30		30	180
	Electricity			240			240			240			240	960
	Water			50			50			50			50	200
	Stationery	42	42	42	42	42	42	42	42	42	42	42	42	504
	Travel	70	70	70	70	70	70	70	70	70	70	70	70	840
	Sundries	75	75	75	75	75	75	75	75	75	75	75	75	900
	Total indirect costs	1,562	1,592	2,227	1,592	1,562	1,882	1,562	1,592	2,227	1,592	1,562	1,882	20,834
Gives:	Net profit	1,850	1,820	1,185	12,045	3,348	3,028	3,138	1,253	618	1,253	18,898	2,023	50,459

The business plan shows that you estimate that you will make a net profit of 50,459 NU during the 12 months. Out of this you have to pay yourself, pay interest on loans, make loan repayments and build up the reserves of the business so as to finance future expansion and to have funds in reserve in case of unexpected events.

The above is a simple example of how a business plan is drawn up. It starts with the sales forecast and then the production plan. It takes account of changes in personnel and other changes (e.g. in prices) and brings them all together to form a general plan for your business for the next "planning period", which is usually a year.

This business plan has a most important use. It is used to control the operation of your business. Each month you can make up a business report on what actually happened, and compare your actual sales, costs and profits with the figures you wrote into the business plan. Then you can decide what action you must take to improve your business.

▲ CHECK YOUR PROGRESS

IF YOU KNOW WHERE YOU WANT TO GO, YOU CAN CHECK WHETHER YOU ARE ON THE RIGHT TRACK

NEW INVESTMENTS

As time goes on, machinery, equipment, motor vehicles, even buildings, become worn out or out of date. There comes a time when they must be replaced if output is to be kept up. If you are doing well, your business will want to grow. You will need more machines, more vehicles, bigger buildings.

When a machine becomes difficult to operate, makes poor work and begins to break down often, you must ask yourself: "Isn't it time to buy a new one?"

The workers on the machines will soon tell you of the difficulties they have. Your supervisor, if you do not run your workshop yourself, will tell you about breakdowns.

You must also keep good output records. Then it is easy to see when the output of a machine is falling.

OUTPUT CARD ①
TILE PRESS TYPE X

MONTH	N° OF TILES PRODUCED
JAN.	20,000
FEV.	19,000
MAR.	19,000
APR.	18,000
MDY	19,000
JUNE	16,000
JULY	16,000
AUG.	15,000
SEP.	14,000
OCT.	14,000
NOV.	
DEC.	

WHEN YOU KEEP GOOD OUTPUT RECORDS YOU CAN SEE WHEN OUTPUT IS FALLING

Example

Suppose you are the owner of a tile press which has been regularly making 1,000 tiles a day. During the past year the workers on the press complain of difficulties; there are more spoiled tiles.

Breakdowns and repair bills are getting bigger, and the daily output is now only about 700 tiles a day.

You sell the tiles for 2 NU a tile. In the past you made and sold 5,000 tiles in a five-day week, which brought in 10,000 NU a week. Now, with an average of 700 tiles a day, the machine is making only 3,500 tiles a week. Income is down to 7,000 NU a week, so you are losing 3,000 NU a week, or 144,000 NU in a 48-week year. That is a lot of money. If you used to make 30 per cent profit on an output of 5,000 tiles a week (i.e. 3,000 NU), you do not make a profit any more. The time has come to replace your press.

You must first get information about new tile presses of different makes and compare their prices and outputs. It helps if you can see some of the presses in operation or learn about them from people who have used them.

A modern press will certainly do better than an old press like the one you have. If the press you like costs 150,000 NU, including shipping, import duties and installation, and can make 6,000 tiles in a five-day week, you will get 2,500 *more* tiles a week than you are getting from your old press, i.e. 5,000 NU a week more and 240,000 NU *more* in a year (48 weeks).

This is a great difference. You will be able to recover the money which you invested in the new machine in two or three years, and costs or repair will also be much lower. You will have fewer breakdowns and higher-quality tiles.

BEFORE MAKING ANY INVESTMENT:

- GET INFORMATION
- COMPARE PRICES AND OUTPUTS
- TRY TO SEE THE EQUIPMENT YOU WANT IN OPERATION

Note: Every case is not as clear as this one, which has been made simple. That is why it is very important to keep good records of output, repair bills and so on for each important machine. Only then do you have good information in order to be able to compare old with new and decide when to replace.

CHOOSING NEW MACHINES

Not many owners of small businesses have the technical knowledge to be able to make a choice between many different machines, which may be much more modern than the ones they know.

DO YOU HAVE THE KNOWLEDGE TO JUDGE WHAT IS BEST FOR YOU?

They are often persuaded by sales representatives to buy machines and other equipment which are too big or in other ways not the best for their needs. Sales representatives may be more interested in making the biggest sale than in selling exactly what is best for you. Be on your guard! If you choose badly, you are wasting your money.

WHAT YOU WANT

WHAT THE SALES REPRESENTATIVE WANTS TO SELL YOU

When you buy an important new machine, you are buying not only for today but for the future. Some of the questions you must ask yourself are:

- Do you want a machine or piece of equipment of the same type, and with the same output, as the one you have?

- Do you think you will have the same or a bigger demand for your products in the next five years? How much bigger?

- Is there a newer process, cheaper and perhaps easier to operate (with less-skilled workers), which is now used instead of your old machine and process? Have you looked at it?

- Can your workers operate the new machine without additional training? If not, where can they be trained? Locally? At the manufacturer's business?

- Will the new machine work with your present raw materials? If not, will you be able to buy the new type of raw materials easily, and at what cost?

- Is there any company in your country or nearby which has the new machine or process you are thinking of buying? Can you go and look at it when it is working and learn about it?

Once you have got quotations for your new machine or equipment, you should:

- get written guarantees of output and quality of production. Even then, check with someone who has used the machine;

- check on the delivery date. Do not trust promises that look too good;

- buy enough spare parts and make sure they are the ones you will need most. Find out if you can get servicing and spares in your country or from nearby;

- obtain detailed instructions on operation and maintenance;

- make sure you get the best terms for installation and start-up;

- try to obtain advice from a Small Business Centre, a technical college or a consultant.

> *Remember:* Buying new capital equipment is a very serious matter and if you are not careful you can waste a great deal of money – *your* money!

ENDPIECE

What we have said in this *Handbook* is:

- Earn more profit by getting more *money in* and paying less *money out*.

- Remember that better selling increases *money in.* Better buying reduces *money out*.

- Reduce waste – waste of material, time, labour and money.

- Keep good records of sales, costs and production. That is how you can control your business.

- Know your costs and you can set your prices. Then you can compete better.

- What matters is what gives your customers satisfaction.

- Remember that profit is an idea but cash is a fact. Make sure you always have enough cash in your business.

- Organise your office efficiently – it is your business image.

- Plan for the future and you will avoid unpleasant surprises.